AN HOUR WITH JESUS

AN HOUR WITH JESUS

Published by:

The Riehle Foundation
P.O. Box 7
Milford, OH 45150
513-576-0032

Nihil Obstat: Rev. Ralph J. Lawrence
March 10, 1994

Imprimatur: ✠ Most Rev. Carl K. Moeddel
Auxiliary Bishop
Archdiocese of Cincinnati
March 15, 1994

Published by The Riehle Foundation
For additional copies, write:

The Riehle Foundation
P.O. Box 7
Milford, Ohio 45150
513-576-0032

Library of Congress Catalog Card No.: 94-065655

ISBN: 1-877678-27-9

Scriptural excerpts from *The New American Bible,* and *The Jerusalem Bible.*

TABLE OF CONTENTS

SUGGESTED USE FOR THIS BOOK

This book is being offered to all those who wish to spend quiet time in prayer before the Lord, particularly in adoration of the Blessed Sacrament. The book is composed of four sections:

PART I is composed of meditations. It is suggested that the reader give special attention to this section. If more personalized prayer is desired, as opposed to structured prayer such as the Rosary, this section can cover an entire one hour period.

A series of meditations are provided and encourage your own personal input, reflection, or response. Prayers are added after some of the meditations. Others allow for your own prayer in response, or, in the silence of your heart, Our Lord's response to you.

PART II Consists of a series of prayers covering a multitude of topics. Included are both traditional and more contemporary prayers. They are available to fill out the time frame for your visit with the Lord.

PART III offers a prepared format designed to cover a period of one hour with Our Lord. It includes a Scriptural Rosary on the passion and death of Jesus, a litany in honor of His Most Sacred Heart, a chaplet of Divine Mercy, and periods for personalized prayers and meditations, found in parts I and II of the book.

PART IV provides a prepared format for a second hour, using some of the above criteria, and adding additional prayers.

Come to me all you who labor and are heavily burdened, and I will refresh you and give you peace of soul.
(*Mt.* 11:28-29).

OPENING PRAYER

I have come, my Lord, to be with You, to recall the great mystery of faith: Your true presence in the consecrated bread of life. I come to adore You, Jesus, by acts of faith, hope, and love; to express sorrow for my sins; to make reparation for the sins of the whole world; to thank You for Your blessings and gifts, so many of which we take for granted; and to present to You my needs, my fears, and my desire for You to govern my life.

I pray to the Holy Spirit of light and truth to fill my heart and enkindle the fire of Your divine love. I also ask our Blessed Mother to be with me as I visit her Divine Son.

Lord, I may not be able to find all the words to express what is really in my heart. I may be distracted and perhaps feel a weariness. Regardless, I kneel in silence before You, knowing that You **know** my innermost thoughts and desires.

I come to renew my personal love for You, and to attempt to rededicate my life to You. Please touch my heart and my soul with Your peace.

PART I

MEDITATIONS

Before the Blessed Sacrament

Following is a series of meditations on a variety of subjects. Included is the opportunity for you, the reader, to reflect and to provide your own input to the meditation.

A prayer of response is then provided for some of the meditations. Others ask for your prayer in response. Several provide a possible response from Our Lord.

MEDITATION:
HOW TO PRAISE YOU LORD?

How should we praise You, Jesus? In Your humility and love for us You choose to be present to us in this hidden form. It doesn't allow for a lot of fanfare, does it? But then again, Your whole life wasn't built around any fanfare. It just seems that the whole world should be more aware of Your presence here. Shouldn't all come in praise and adoration? You are their Saviour. How can we praise You enough, Lord?

What if it was the President that was actually here? Would this building be filled? Or a great movie star? Or a professional athlete? Or even the Pope? Would crowds jam the building? Would the media be here, cameras rolling? Applause? Would they bow if it were the Queen of England who was present here? And yet—those are only people! You are our Saviour, Our Lord. And only a few come! Why?

Dear Jesus! How incredibly indifferent and fickle we are! How little our faith. If You announced You were coming here in person, visible to all, no structure could hold the crowds. Every nation in the world would respond, every form of media would be a mere instrument of communication in Your hands. All would bow—and kneel—and sing, and ask for blessings, healing, more forgiveness. They would all come—if they could see You.

The mystery of Your sovereign existence Lord! The mystery of Your actually suffering death for us, of Your forgiveness, Your love. And still You choose to meet us in this hidden, humble form! How do we respond to You?

REFLECTION

PRAYER:

All praise and honor and glory to You, Lord Jesus Christ!

Praise You Jesus—in thanksgiving for my existence.

Praise You Jesus—for Your Love for me, for Your forgiveness.

Praise You Jesus—for Your suffering, Your passion, Your crucifixion for our sins, and for our redemption.

Praise You Jesus—for becoming man for my sake. For actually showing us how to live, for providing us with the path to follow You to eternity.

Praise You Jesus—for continuing to love us in spite of our sinfulness.

Praise You Jesus—for Your acceptance of me in spite of my indifference, in spite of my lack of conversion, in spite of my love for the materialistic world, in spite of my human pride.

Praise You Jesus—for each new beating heart, for each life You create, for each willing mother to produce it.

Praise You Jesus—for giving us Your Church, Your Pope, for Your sacraments—for sending the Holy Spirit as You promised, to guide and direct us in Your truths.

Praise You Jesus—for giving to me personally, the opportunities and challenges You have placed in my life. For the gift of loving, forgiving, believing and giving. I ask Your forgiveness for all those occasions where I have been indifferent to those gifts.

Praise You Jesus—for giving me, and each of us, one of Your angels for our protectors. Dear Jesus, how seldom we think of, or recognize, the presence of our guardian angels.

Praise You Jesus—for giving us Your Mother, Mary Immaculate, as our special mother, our spiritual director. Forgive my indifference in recognizing her presence, or for not truly listening for her direction or seeking her intercession.

Praise You Jesus—for making Yourself available to me in the Eucharist—the Heavenly bread—for being the Way, the Truth, and the Life.

Praise You Jesus—for everything created on this earth, in the sky above, in the seas below. Praise You Jesus—for life. For Yours, for mine, for all.

Praise You Jesus—for Your willingness to manifest Your true and awesome presence in the mere form of a host.

Lord Jesus! I bow before You! Increase my faith, my trust.

MEDITATION:
WHAT DO YOU SEE? WHAT DOES HE SEE?

Jesus! My Saviour, my Lord! I look at that host—at You truly present in the Blessed Sacrament. But what do I see? My mind wanders. What image is created? Do I really need to see some actual image of You?

What image do You see in looking at me? Lord, perhaps I really don't want that question answered. A sinner? Indifference? Lack of love, lack of faith? A life created by You to honor, serve and love You—still unconverted? Might You see someone coming to give You just time, or lip service? You said that in Your Gospels, Lord: *"These people honor me with their lips, but their hearts are far from me."*

Should I see You in Your glory, Lord—the risen Christ now at the right hand of the Father? Or in a manger at Bethlehem? Your crucifixion, Your pain, Your suffering? Should I see a compassionate Jesus? A God of justice in judgment?

What do You see in looking at me Lord? I can't see the real, human image of You. Do you just see the human image of me? Maybe, I would prefer if You saw me in some other form too. But You said that You came to call sinners. Then, Lord Jesus, I bring You my sins. Heal in me whatever You see that needs healing.

Please see me as one who comes to address the Saviour!

PAUSE AND REFLECT

PRAYER:

Jesus! Do You see how often my pride, my ego, has turned my best intentions into fits of failure or pain? Please send Your Spirit to fill me with a true sense of humility.

Jesus! Do You see how often my failure to forgive has resulted in just making matters worse, in increasing resentment? Send Your Spirit to fill me with the sense of forgiveness You exhibited from the cross.

Jesus! Do You recognize how often my indifference has left You out of any accomplishments I may have achieved—seemingly on my own? Send Your Spirit to fill me with an abandonment to Your will.

Jesus! Do You recognize how often my lack of love and concern has left so many people unfulfilled and neglected. Please send Your Spirit to fill me with a sense of love and caring for all of Your creatures.

Jesus! Do You see how often my lack of faith and trust has blamed You for the failures and frustrations in my life? Send Your Spirit to fill me with a sense of true belief in You.

Jesus! Do You recognize how often my lack of submission to Your commandments has added to my problems? Please send Your Spirit to fill me with complete obedience and a willingness to give You control in my life.

Jesus! Do You see how often my place in eternity is jeopardized through my faults?

You recognize all these things. Please help me to.

MEDITATION: SILENCE

What is true silence? It means more than just the absence of sound. You are silent, Lord. Ever present, but without fanfare, without noise, nothing added to enhance Your presence, Your beauty, Your majesty.

Lord Jesus, how do I find true silence, especially in Your presence? Help me to become an empty vessel—a truly empty shell, void of all distractions, all thoughts, and in total quietness. Then I think I could really hear and feel You speaking to me. Then I could be silent and You could talk.

But I can't seem to reach that point all by myself, Lord. I need Your help. Send the Holy Spirit, as You promised, to create that empty vessel and to then fill me with those gifts. I need to hear Your words, seek Your will, accept Your love and forgiveness. Show me how to find true silence.

Is it in the heart and mind, Lord? Is it a true mental and spiritual stillness, not based on any physical attributes? Lord, that I might concentrate only on you; then my heart and mind might find that stillness.

PAUSE AND REFLECT

PRAYER:

(My response)

MEDITATION:
THANK YOU, LORD

My Jesus! I need to spend time here thanking You. I want to find simple words, that can convey my thanks for all You have given me in my life. I realize the importance of praise and adoration, and recognition of Your presence. I do not come because of a symbol of Your presence. I believe You truly are present. And aside from giving You the praise You so worthily deserve, I also realize a need to thank You.

Words can be difficult, Lord. Here I sit, actually in Your presence! My ego facing Your humility. My pride facing Your forgiveness. My indifference and Your commitment of love, offering Your life, on my behalf. My sins, Your crucifixion. Earthly pain linked to eternal reign.

How do I thank You, Lord, for this profound gift of accepting my presence here—this awesome gift where the creature is allowed to spend intimate time with the Lord God? I know I don't merit such a gift. I'm here as a sinner. One way or the other, I'm still crucifying You each day. Still, I come. Thank You for accepting me.

Lord, there are so, so many others more worthy than I that could be here to keep You company. So many who have been more faithful than I. Would You be more pleased at their presence? Or is that why I am here? Are You giving me this special opportunity to talk with You because You need me here more than someone else? Am I more in need of conversion? That means trying harder to put my life in Your hands, doesn't it? Giving you recognition for all that I am. That's the beginning of offering my "thank you's," Jesus. How long a list that could be!

Lord! Thank You for life. I mean, I do exist. You gave me life. Maybe I haven't always done a very good job of protecting it, or developing it. But, for whatever success or satisfaction I've received, I thank You for it.

I thank You for the love I've found—the people You have put in my life. My friends, Lord, the love I've found there. I never tell them.

I thank You for the people I've been able to touch in my life. You give us so many opportunities to add something to someone else's life. How few times we capitalize on them. Too often they are here and then gone—lost.

I thank You, Lord, for my family. How many more opportunities You give us through families, Lord! How many are missed! How much more love could have been nurtured. Thank You for the chance to do it now, and in the future.

I thank You for giving me life during this time Lord, and in this part of the world. "There but for the grace of God, go I." It could have been in times and places of war and desolation. Or where there is open persecution against Your people, Your Church. Or regions of total famine, and complete poverty. It all could have been so much worse.

Lord Jesus! Forgive my apathy, my indifference, my failure to simply offer a daily "thank you." Who am I, Lord, to think I will have all this forever—that I will never die, or get any older than I am?

I thank You for creation. For every tree and flower. For every river and ocean. I thank You for everything I take for granted every day, often times never even seeing—the sun, the sky, the air we breathe, laughter and joy, the food You provide, the children You create.

I guess I thank You most of all for Your compassion, Your forgiveness, Your mercy. The more I think of things to thank You for, the more I'm aware of Your mercy—because I have so seldom expressed my thanks.

You said You came to forgive sins. Lord, I need You

to forgive mine. Why do we always recognize that need for forgiveness after the fact, sometimes when it is too late? Lord, how many of my family and relatives are now gone from this world? How many I have forgotten about. How many opportunities You give me to spread Your word, Your love. All those "could have beens" and "should have dones." How many didn't I do. And I guess, Lord, many of us are still in that pattern. Thank You Jesus for continuing to place new opportunities before me. Thank You for making me more aware that I need to be a disciple.

Thank You especially for my spouse, and for my children. It is hard to visualize life without certain people in it, Lord. Thank You for the love they provide, the joy, and even sometimes the pain.

Jesus! Thank You for being my salvation, for dying for me. If You hadn't, You wouldn't be available to me in the Eucharist; You wouldn't be present in that host. Thank You!

REFLECT

PRAYER:

(My response)

MEDITATION:
HEALING

Your people seek Your face, Lord. We can't see Your face, but most of us believe. We try. We struggle. How often we fail, but we try. We get up again.

Should life be such a struggle? I mean, don't You see all this suffering, Lord? All this pain? Should the innocent always bear the brunt of it?

Lord, I need to ask You about all the homeless. About all those who live in total poverty. And the hungry of the world! It seems there are so many. Persecution is still there, in so many ways, in so many parts of the world.

How can we better protect Your little children, Jesus? All the neglect, the violence, the abuse they suffer? We haven't really improved Your world much, have we?

And how many of us are ill, Lord? As if we don't have enough sickness and disease, we keep creating more on our own. Jesus, there are so many who suffer, who need physical healing. Just as many more that suffer emotionally, spiritually.

Couldn't You have sent a great leader for the world, one who could lead the world as You wish? After all, it is Your creation. Couldn't You have sent someone to cure cancer? How many more must perish from this illness? Or AIDS? Couldn't You have sent a great medical leader? A political leader to balance economies and eliminate hunger? Is there truly one here who can unite all Your people, Lord?

You walked this earth, lived a human life, Jesus. Yet, You could make the blind see, the cripples walk. You cured the lepers, and even raised Lazarus from the dead. You converted sinners instantly. You multiplied the loaves and fishes. Our Lord and Redeemer, You alone have the power. You can cure all.

Then again, maybe You did send a great healer, a great leader, a great peacemaker. Maybe You did create souls to come to the aid of Your anguished people. What if we eliminated their lives through abortion? You do continue to have Your Mother, the Immaculate Mary, visit the earth to try to change the hearts of Your people. Not many wish to hear what she has to say, do they? Not many wish to accept the directions of Your Pope.

You have created a proud and arrogant people, Lord. Sin and violence and rejection of Your grace produce sickness and pain. I guess it will all disappear when we finally turn back to You—and then **WE** will take credit for the victory.

Dear Jesus! The world needs Your healing all over again!

REFLECT

(Your own petitions on healing)

PRAYER:

Jesus! I believe that You came into the world for sinners; that You came to heal mankind. I believe You are the Divine Physician, and that You can cure all of our ills. I believe in Your words: *Ask and you shall receive, seek and you shall find, knock and it shall be opened to you.* Heal, Lord Jesus!

Jesus! There is no sin and no illness that You cannot eliminate with Your almighty word. There is no wound You cannot heal. Lord, Jesus! Heal in me whatever needs healing. Heal my body of this ___(illness)___, and restore me to health, to serve and praise You, and You alone, as the source of my health.

Jesus! I lift up to You all who suffer with physical infirmity, especially ______(name)______. Turn Your face to those who come to You in their need. Restore their strength. Remove every tumor, every disease, every dysfunction. As You healed the cripples and the lepers because of their faith, so touch these, now, faithful and devoted to Your word. Heal, Lord Jesus!

Jesus! Touch those who, in their suffering, do not know You, do not have faith. Through Your healing, create a new, great light in their souls, and a zeal to go out and proclaim that You alone are Lord!

Jesus! I lift up to You all those who live in a life of addiction, whose free will has been diluted. Touch all those who suffer from drugs, alcohol, nicotine, sexual abuse. Loose their body and soul from every evil influence.

Jesus! Heal all those who have been deceived by Satan and his evil legions. All those caught in various forms of idolatry. Those whose lives are filled with hatred and unforgiveness, who worship materialistic and worldly idols.

Jesus! Heal all those, so many, who know not love. Remove from their hearts all remnants of a painful heritage. Cure their souls of any and all burdens they carry, including those carried forth from childhood. Remove anything in them that blocks their capacity to love.

Jesus! Heal those who cannot forgive, or those who are shackled to painful memories. You, Lord Jesus, who forgave from Your cross, grant the gift of forgiveness to all those who suffer from past hurts or the mistakes of others. Expel all memories that are painful to them and that block loving relationships with You and with others. Forgive and eliminate all envy, jealousy, mistrust, and fear. Especially within families, Lord.

Jesus! I lift up to You all who suffer emotional illness. Those burdened with personality difficulty and neurosis. Heal them of depression and grant forgiveness to them and to any others who may have caused their burden.

Free them from any thought of suicide, or from any evil spirit who preys on their illness.

Jesus! Hear the cries of the children! Give special attention to the little ones who suffer—from illness, from hunger, from poverty, from abuse. Heal those who are responsible for them and have failed in any way to provide for their needs, especially for their spiritual needs; that they might know that You exist, and of Your special love for them. Jesus! Heal families. Cure whatever might exist in any family that is a source of abuse to a spouse, and especially to a child.

Jesus! I lift up all people, all nations, all races. You, as the Prince of Peace, can eliminate their prejudice, their hatreds, their misunderstandings, their greed. Cover all nations with a zest for love, forgiveness, and peace. Heal Lord Jesus!

Jesus! Heal Your Church.

Dear God, I praise You and thank You for responding to me. May Your healing love pour out on me, on my family, on our specific illnesses. May it touch all who suffer, or who need special healing. May it pour out upon all the world through Jesus, Our Lord. Heal, Lord Jesus!

MEDITATION:
JESUS! WHO ARE YOU?

Lord, do we sometimes see You as some mythical figure? It's hard to recognize that just another human being would spend His life trying to convert and save mankind, and accept torture and crucifixion on our behalf. Then, to think that the God-man actually did that! Who would be expected to do that in this world? That kind of sacrifice?

The Saviour! The Promised Messiah! Wouldn't He have come in royalty? In splendor, and with great worldly power? Why didn't You?

Instead, the whole story of Your life is forgiveness and love, Lord. All the Gospels spell it out. And what did Your people offer You in return, Lord?

Some see Satan as a mythical figure too. They can't fathom the reality of Hell, or grasp the sense of time that "eternity" conveys. Lord, how many people have asked You if there wasn't a better way to do all that? A better way to accomplish our redemption? Did You have to come in the form of "a nobody," to be crucified by the very people You came to save? Can we ever fathom the depth of that kind of love and commitment—the Creator submitting to the creature?

Dear Jesus! How can we understand the depths of Your humility, Your compassion?

REFLECT

(Add your own meditation)

PRAYER:

My Jesus! Does it really matter? God's ways are not our ways. You are indeed a mysterious God. But then, how else could we understand Your compassion, Your love, if You didn't provide it to us on our own level, using our values, our standards?

My Lord! You chose to come to this world in the most simple and humble way. You lived in poverty. There was no great army, no kingdom, no golden chariot, no legion of angels. You chose to come to us through the Blessed Virgin Mary. God picked a human being to bring the Lord of Lords into the world, and simply asked for her willingness, her fiat, her "yes."

Dear Jesus! How long have You waited for my fiat? How patient and merciful You are, waiting for my commitment, while I often live in indifference, oblivious to Your presence. Yet, all You really ask for is my "yes." Give me the grace to love You in return. Give me the grace to call on Your Mother as my example and to follow her fiat with my own.

Jesus Christ, I believe in You. I believe in Your true presence. I believe You, the Saviour of the world, gave Your life for my redemption.

MEDITATION:
THE LORD NEVER CHANGES

Lord God, for thousands of years mankind has paid You homage. For century upon century Your people have come to You in their need. Help us to recognize that You never change, Lord. You are the hidden Jesus in the tabernacle, in the Blessed Sacrament. You are Yahweh of old, the God of the Old Testament. You are Jesus Christ, God made man. You are the unfathomable mystery of the Holy Trinity. You are the eternal God who always was, who always will be. And You are the saving Jesus who came to redeem mankind. Millions upon millions of people have passed by on this earth on their journey to eternal life, and You were there, present and available to each of them.

It is we who have changed, Lord. Your planet earth has seen incredible change. The advancements and intelligence of mankind are almost beyond belief. Look how far we have advanced, Lord! But all for the better? Mankind changes from century to century, our standard of living leaps dramatically with every passing generation. Look how we have improved the quality of life, Lord!

But we keep killing each other, destroying each other, creating new sicknesses. We are ever changing Lord, except in our sinfulness.

Humans change. They come and they go. But You Lord, are eternal. Ever the same. Ever the same God. Your mercy and Your forgiveness last for endless years. Your love for Your creatures, in spite of their sinfulness, goes on for countless centuries. Through our changing futility, help us to hang on to Your eternal promises.

PAUSE AND REFLECT

(Add your response, your prayer)

MEDITATION:
OUR PRIVATE WORLD

Here we are in our world, Lord. In our good days and in our misery. In our suffering and pain. In our ups and downs. We keep searching.

Peace never seems to be quite within reach. It never truly comes. We're always working toward getting somewhere, but never quite make it. All we get is older—and not always wiser. The end of the rainbow is always just around the corner. Or is it?

And all these material things, Lord? They don't last. And it seems they never can guarantee the satisfaction they promise. We always want more. The money doesn't seem to be able to buy happiness, and it sure can't buy health. The only thing we are certain of is our death—and we don't want to face that either. What really counts? How do we really achieve peace? Contentment?

PAUSE AND REFLECT

PRAYER:

Lord, it seems like we can't really achieve what we strive for here on our own. It's all hidden in a fog or sealed up in plastic wrap that you can never completely get off. It's all a facade, Lord. It isn't real, or lasting—or satisfying, or peaceful.

Jesus! Here we are, stumbling around, sometimes in misery, ever searching, ever seeking. We become blinded by our own greed and pride, systematically destroying Your creation—and each other—trying to rationalize your laws to fit our needs. We wind up rejecting your gifts and graces by trying to substitute them for "our rights" and momentary pleasures.

Dear Lord Jesus, open our eyes that we might see that You are real, that Your love and forgiveness is real and is all we truly need. Help us to realize that Satan and evil are real as well, and that eternity truly exists. All those things we're searching for? Your words covered them all, Lord, in the Bible. We only need to search them out. Jesus, forgive our arrogance and lack of belief.

MEDITATION:
YOUR CHURCH, LORD!

Lord Jesus, may all who come before You in the Blessed Sacrament of the Altar, at any time, anywhere in the world, come to also offer prayer, sacrifice and petition for priests, and for Your Church.

The evil one is attempting to ravage Your Church. How indifferent many of Your people are. Many are not even aware of this current spiritual battle, that it is evil that attempts to destroy Your priesthood.

Why is there such division? So much confusion and discontent? Have Your Commandments really changed, Lord? Are Your Scriptures obsolete? Are we remiss in not standing up for Your Church, and for Your shepherds? Does the advancement of civilization really require a reinterpretation of Your words? Did You really give us the authority to teach our children, define sin, and guarantee salvation, based only on our own conscience? Omnipotent God in Heaven, take back control of Your Church, and once again, send the Paraclete to touch Your priests.

Show us what we need! Where we are lacking or misdirected. Unite Your people in support of the Magisterium of Your Church. Renew our teachers with a zeal and commitment to teach only Your truths.

PAUSE AND REFLECT. WHERE WOULD WE BE WITHOUT THE CHURCH?

PRAYER:

Jesus, in this sinful and violent world, we recognize the needs of Your priests. In the face of over-bearing worldly concerns and temptations, give them strength to be faithful to their vocation. In a world that openly scorns Your truths, send the Holy Spirit to fill the hearts and minds of Your priests with acceptance of these truths. Expose the false teaching prevalent in Your Church today, and strengthen commitment to Church authority in the minds of all of Your priests.

Lord, we pray for Your bishops and all Church authority. Give them the courage and conviction to stand firm and proclaim Your teachings. We pray that they will find renewed vigor for the salvation of the souls of their flock, and less concern with worldly needs.

We pray for all religious and brothers. Lord Jesus, give special blessings to the sisters of all orders, so often neglected and taken for granted in their vocations. Renew them and their commitments, and look favorably on all of their needs.

Lord, we pray for vocations. May the Holy Spirit touch many young men and women with a hunger for Your service. Perhaps more importantly, we need them to be taught and nurtured with the true teachings of Your Church. Lord, renew the teaching institutions of Your Church. Come, Lord Jesus!

MEDITATION:
LIFE'S GOALS AND OUR NEEDS

Lord, we were created with needs, with goals. You gave us a life complete with free will, with intellect, with talents. But sometimes our desire to control, to decide, to succeed, only further develops our own weakness. Our failures can then block Your grace, Your blessings. The pride and ego of Your creatures, Lord, can extinguish the light of Your mercy and compassion. We always think we can produce light, but often we create a dark fog that hides frustrations and disappointments.

Are my goals wrong, Lord? Am I being deceived by what I think my needs are? But they seem so obvious, so realistic. My family relationships—seeing mistakes being made by those I love. Seeing my own mistakes and failures that hurt them. And my financial needs. The success I crave, the peace I can't really find. Is all that wrong? And my health! I can't control what might happen.

And mostly, the unknown. I realize I will die. But there is still so much to do. I'm not ready. I don't know what You have in store for me.

(Include your input, your meditation, your response)

PRAYER:

My hidden Jesus. I need You. I need You. Give me the strength and courage to proclaim my weakness. Help me to recognize that acceptance of my weakness enables Your strength. Help me to seek Your control, Your grace, Your guidance. I need to be willing to put more into Your hands, to recognize there is so much I am helpless to change.

I need You, Lord. Give me the grace to be able to ask You to control my life—for You to decide what I really need, what really is important. I believe in You, Lord Jesus. I relinquish control. I put it in Your hands. I believe in Your mercy, Your forgiveness, Your love for me. I believe You will provide what is best for me. You have promised us as much.

Mary, Mother of my Saviour, pray with me and for me, that I might develop your sense of humility, your obedience, your total trust and acceptance in the will of God. Ultimately, it is my only goal, my only need.

MEDITATION:
JESUS! ARE YOU REALLY THERE?

We come and see an artistic adornment. A host. Is that You? We see Your crucifix, Your image on a cross. It is familiar to us. We identify with that image. It is You, Lord. But are we really kneeling in Your presence?

We kneel here and see a representation of You in total suffering—a martyred God. Shouldn't we be awed by Your splendor Lord, overwhelmed by Your majesty, power, and greatness? Shouldn't we see You as the glorified Lord of Lords, and King of Kings—in a brilliant white light, majestic and beautiful beyond belief?

Lord, if we truly kneel before You, and if You are the Creator and we just the creatures, kneeling here in Your presence, shouldn't we be in some massive hall, some great room? I mean, shouldn't there be twenty foot high ceilings, and great columns, and marble floors and walls? Isn't there supposed to be plush carpet, and a high throne with a gold chair? Shouldn't there be Heavenly choirs of soft music—an array of angels everywhere? And great choirs singing Your praises?

How should we approach You, Lord, in Your hidden presence?

REFLECT

(Add your own response)

MIGHT HIS RESPONSE BE:

I choose to come before you as the image of your rejection—as a reminder to you of my suffering. I choose to be present to you in this hidden form, a host, to allow you to search me out, to develop your trust and belief.

For all too soon you will see me in that great hall, in that brilliant light, on that golden throne. And you will be overwhelmed by my majesty. But then you will be kneeling before me to receive my judgment. Are you ready?

I shall allow you to prepare yourself first—by coming to me here—to seek me out, to express your love, your belief, to ask my forgiveness. In the great hall, it will then be too late.

MEDITATION:
HOW DOES HE SPEAK?

My Lord, God! Do You actually speak? People come. They pray. They try to seek You out, and they bring You their needs. They offer prayer. They believe, Lord. I believe. I am here because I believe You are here. But will I hear You speak? I sit here in silence, listening for Your words. But I'm not sure I sense communication. Am I doing this right, Lord?

You've actually spoken to Your people, Lord, to Your prophets and saints. Some others claim they hear Your voice. Do I need to pray more? Or say less? What is it I should hear? Or feel? Wouldn't all Your people immediately convert their lives if they just heard Your voice? You could change the world in an instant if we actually saw You! Do You actually speak, Lord? I accept the fact that You shouldn't actually speak to me. I admit to my failures, and I confess that I am not worthy. But, if You actually spoke...

Do we really even need to hear You speak? If we actually heard You, would sin suddenly disappear? Have Your people always looked for signs and wonders, Lord? In all of the centuries, how many people fit the term, "doubting Thomas?" But You asked us to come to You, Lord. You asked us to speak with You. If You actually spoke...

PAUSE AND REFLECT

(Add your own prayer in response)

AND MIGHT HIS RESPONSE BE:

Yes, I speak. But you try to hear my words only through your human ears. Your heart must be still.

I spoke. My words are all printed in a book. Do you

read it? I actually walked the face of your earth, and spoke my words to my people. Many rejected them, and their persecution of me resulted in my death—for your salvation.

Yes, I spoke through my prophets, my saints. I still do. I speak also through my Pope. Do my people listen to him?

But most importantly, I speak directly to you. I need for you to be silent to hear me; to be a completely empty vessel. For you see, I speak through your mind, and most importantly, through your heart. In your meditation, in your contemplation, in your silent recognition of my presence, I respond to you. It will be the thoughts you suddenly sense in your mind. It will be the truths you painfully accept in your heart regarding your unworthiness. The ache you feel for serenity, peace, and comfort, that frustration you sense struggling for constant control of your own destiny, your desire to actually hear me, these are all the words of your God speaking to you. If your heart and soul are truly silent, your thoughts will be my words to you.

One thing more, I need you to give me your heart unconditionally. You must truly commit to give me your love, just as I give you mine. Then our hearts speak to each other. No words are needed!

MEDITATION:
THE SPLENDOR OF YOUR GLORY, LORD!

We never have been able to capture the magnificence of Your glory, Lord. Your incomparable beauty. The splendor of Your majesty. In prose, in printed word, in art, in song—Your people continually try to convey an image of Your beauty, but it all falls short. It remains for us to get to where You are before we will ever be able to comprehend it.

You do give us glimpses, Lord. You do allow us to make some sort of comparison through the work of Your hand, Your creation. The beauty of Your creation comes in many forms; it is visible to us each day. I wonder why we see so little of it?

It is there in the sun, the sky, the ocean, the majestic beauty of the mountain, or just a single tree. It is in the babbling brook, the wooded glen, the forest, the great formations of rock and canyon.

How many different flowers did You create, Lord? All that color and beauty. I see the different birds come to the bird feeders—just common everyday birds—but there are so many different kinds, so many different colors. How did You make all the leaves turn so many colors in the Fall?

Your beauty is in every child, Lord. In their innocence and laughter. In every baby's smile. Who can ever comprehend the complexities of the human body, the wonder of Your creation.

A mere glimpse of Your majesty is available to us through the liturgies, in the choirs with songs of praise. It is there in the architecture of so many churches erected in Your honor.

Maybe Your beauty is most available to us through love. We can't see this the same way we view the mountain, but it is still more profound. It combines peace, and joy, and happiness, and a spirit of giving—and forgiving. Those things are all part of You, aren't they?

Your works are great indeed, my God. Help us to better see the splendor and beauty of Your glory.

PAUSE AND REFLECT

PRAYER:

Jesus! It's a pleasant task, trying to comprehend Your beauty, Your majesty. Still, it is an impossible one. Simply give us the grace to offer praise, and adoration. Fill us with joy at the wonder of Your awesome creation. Give sight to our hearts as well as our eyes, that through our hearts we might see the splendor of Your glory.

Give us the grace to be able to rejoice in the beauty of the world You have given us.

Give us the grace to be able to see the beauty of our own soul—without the stain of sin—created to spend eternity with You as part of Your glory.

Give us the grace to see, in all things, light instead of darkness, joy instead of pain, love instead of hatred, fulfillment instead of frustration.

Dear Jesus! The true measure of Your beauty, Your majesty, Your glory, will only be found in Heaven. Until I come home to You, I will never be able to fathom it. You told us as much. You told us that eye has not seen and ear has not heard what You have planned for those who love You.

Lord Jesus, increase my love for You.

MEDITATION
COME HOME WITH ME, LORD

Here, it is so quiet, Lord. I love the quiet. It helps me absorb the idea that You are here with me, that You and I are really visiting. Sometimes it seems so very noisy away from here that I can't find a still place to even try to seek You out. You are elusive in the noise!

Still, I can hear the climate control systems of the building. I can hear the distant sounds of cars, sirens, playing children, barking dogs. These sounds are worldly background. In your human form, You experienced all these noises, Lord. You know of the distinctions.

At moments like these, I can even hear my heart beating. I can hear each time I inhale and exhale. Do You breathe in Your glorified body? Do You breathe with me, Lord? Does Your Sacred Heart actually beat? Can our hearts beat together, in rhythm with each other?

I listen for the glory of You, our Creator, in the muted sounds surrounding me. Are You in the usual sounds around us? Are You even in my own breathing and beating heart? Are You in the thoughts that pass through my mind? I want You to completely fill every thought I have and everything I am. I want to detect Your presence with my senses.

Here, it is easy for me to think of You, to spill my heart to You. Here the noises are not invasive. But at home, at work, in the stores, in the crowds, the sounds that block my thoughts of You are deafening.

I am comforted here in Your quiet peace. I can more easily perceive Your love here than in the midst of the world's distractions. Come home with me, Lord.

PAUSE AND REFLECT

PRAYER:

Dear Jesus, help us to seek You, even in the noise. Come home with us and point out Your presence in the people and noise around us. Forgive us, Lord, when we lose patience. Help us to remember Your constant love in each encounter in our lives.

Lord God, You are all powerful, all knowing, all loving. You understand our failings. Make up for what is lacking in our nature. Grant us Your peace. Help us to spread Your peace to others around us. Help us to find Your peace in our noise. In only You will we find true peace.

Be at home with us always, Lord. You are our only source of quiet. Let Your quiet and peace fill our hearts so that we find Your presence in all our activities. Remind us of Your presence at the dinner table. Remind us of Your presence as we work and play. Remind us of Your presence as we deal with family issues. Remind us of Your presence in our interactions with our neighbors.

I need You to quiet my fears, to calm my frustrations, to grant me the gift of patience. I need to be aware of You at each moment of my life, as the friend and comforter You are. Come home with me, my sweet Jesus.

MEDITATION:
JOY IN YOUR PRESENCE, LORD

Thank You, dear Jesus, for allowing me to share special time with You. I try to bring You into my day-to-day activities, but I really need a special time to just visit. I am so happy here with You. This little visit will help me find the joy of living in Your love when we can't be together like we are at this moment.

I am constantly amazed at the joy You give me, and the help to cope with the rigors of life. Each day there is something new when You open my eyes to see it.

I revel in You as I see the sun tiptoe into my window in the morning, but I find as much pleasure if, instead, raindrops are dancing on my roof. The smell of freshly turned earth and mowed grass is wonderful! The smells of this world excite me and remind me of You: blooming flowers, dying leaves, an approaching storm, or even logs burning in the fireplace, a sauce simmering on the stove, a powdered baby. I can even smell the snow You send me, Lord, and it quickens my pulse, alerting my senses!

The aches and pains of a hard day of work are a cause of joy if I look for it. I know that physical exhaustion can bring me the deepest sleep. As I drift off, I am joyful, knowing that my head, resting on a pillow, is resting in the crook of Your arm as well.

Even though this is a special time, just for visiting with You, I want to share my excitement about the world with You. You are always with me, and I celebrate Your presence in it. You have shown me, Lord, that the pleasures of this world are best appreciated when You are found in them.

When life doesn't seem to be going well, I still find joy when You remind me that I can be content when I do Your will, even if I experience some pain in the process. You offer obvious joy in beauty, and even help us find it in ugliness. You offer happiness, and You help us find it in the midst of grief. You offer hope, and You help us find it in our despair. You offer elation, and You help us find it in life's doldrums. You offer pure love, and You help us find it through the indifference that surrounds us.

Help me now, Lord, to offer You my heart. I joyfully abandon it to Your loving care. You help me find Your joy in my earthly surroundings; help me find joy in leaving those surroundings behind while I contemplate the wonders of being with You.

PAUSE AND REFLECT

PRAYER:

My precious Lord, Jesus, thank You for being with me in Your Eucharistic presence. Help me to always relish this time we share. Help others to find the joy of living in Your holy will.

Help us also to discover joy in all the gifts You offer us in our earthly existence, whether we perceive them as good or not. Help us to know that Your joy is never ending. You offer it; all we need to do is embrace it.

Dear Lord, please help all the unhappy people in the world. There are so many of Your children who try to find happiness by living in ways which are opposed to Your will. Wake them up, Lord, to the joys of life with You. Open their eyes to the happiness You offer. Take me, Lord, and make me Your ambassador of joy.

(Add your prayer)

MEDITATION:
PASSION AND DEATH OF OUR LORD

(The Stations of the Cross
can be found on page 67.)

The story of Your passion and death has been with us for many centuries. Still, it is difficult, Lord, to truly comprehend the awesome tragedy of that event. How can we really grasp the meaning of it all?

The Promised One, the Messiah, He who was to redeem mankind, was rejected by the people He came to save. The One who came to give all of us life to the fullest was deprived of His. Perhaps, Lord, we wonder why the people of that age could not recognize who You really were. How could they not perceive the signs? Then again, perhaps we don't recognize who You really are today either. We often deny Your presence simply because we can't physically see You. And surely, evil could not be any greater then, than it is now.

But the sequence of it all, Lord! It was not enough to condemn You or reject You, or even take Your life. You had to also be subjected to ridicule, scorn, torture, scourging. They had to make a mockery of Your kingship by pounding a crown of thorns into Your head.

Could it have been that pleasurable for the people to watch You drag the instrument of Your death to the place of crucifixion? What human need was fulfilled witnessing You stumbling, falling, scourged, as you labored to carry a heavy cross past crowds of jeering people? Were some of them the same people you had earlier taught? Or healed?

How can someone truly grasp the agony of crucifixion? The hours of pain? Jesus, can You please help me to understand the reality of Your suffering and death as an act of redemption for me, and for all mankind? Can You please help me to understand the power of Your act of forgiveness from Your cross? True God and True Man! But the True Man suffered true human pain and death—for His people.

PAUSE

(Add your reflection)

PRAYER:

Dear God in Heaven, for all the agony suffered by Your Son, I offer reparation.

Dear God in Heaven, for each of the scourges, the thorns, the nails and the lance used to expel His most precious blood, I offer reparation.

Dear God in Heaven, for the failure of mankind to recognize the time of their salvation, I beg Your mercy.

Dear Jesus, for every sin, past, present and future, committed against Your most Sacred Heart, I seek Your forgiveness.

Dear Jesus, for each time Your name is taken in vain, the source of Your suffering, I seek Your forgiveness.

Dear Jesus, for every soul that refuses to recognize that You are the Lord of Lords, and the King of Kings, I seek Your forgiveness.

Dear Jesus, for every life, including the unborn, that has been taken in an act of violence, extend Your Divine Mercy.

Dear Jesus, for every unrepentant sinner, and for every unforgiven offense, extend Your Divine Mercy.

Dear Jesus, accept our prayers, offered for every pain You endured, for every taunt, for each rejection.

Dear Jesus, permanently write on our hearts the fact that Your greatest suffering was the knowledge that Your passion and death would be in vain for so many.

Lord, have mercy!

MEDITATION:
THE WAY, THE TRUTH, THE LIFE

Three words! Just three words, "way," "truth," and "life," and contained therein are all of our needs and desires for life. I guess our way has not always been Your way, Lord. We've stumbled a lot as a result. It hasn't always worked out like we planned. Yet, You told us that You came so that we might have life to the fullest. It's there if our faith is there, if we follow Your way.

It's difficult to give up control, Lord. It's not just a matter of accepting "Your way"; it seems like it also involves recognizing the truth. You are truth. Your commandments are truth. Truth also brings freedom—if we can accept those truths. And doesn't freedom also bring peace? Isn't that what we are all seeking?

That is all part of life, isn't it? Lord, You are the way, the truth, and the life. Doesn't that also include peace, joy, and freedom? You told us we could achieve those things in following Your words. The world hasn't been able to truly provide those things on its own. It is all so illusive. And yet, You spelled it out for us—that we might have life to the fullest. Lord, isn't it all in the acceptance of You as The Way, The Truth, and The Life?

PAUSE AND REFLECT

PRAYER:

We thank You, Father, for showing us the way by sending us a Saviour. We thank You, Father, for the Truth, crucified for our sins. We thank You, Father, for eternal life, made possible by the Sacrifice of Your Son.

Jesus, You brought us the Good News of salvation. You prepared the way and provided our redemption. All praise to You as our Redeemer.

Jesus, in Your words are truth and life. Give us the grace to follow them instead of merely trying to redirect our conscience to better fit our claimed need. Help us to better recognize that our freedom comes from our acceptance and adherence to Your truths.

Jesus! Your peace, Your love, Your forgiveness, are available to replace our impatience, anger, and frustration. Your truth is available to eliminate our uncertainty and confusion. Your promise of eternal life erases the turmoil of our earthly existence.

Jesus! You came as our Saviour, offering us total redemption through Your crucifixion. All praise and thanksgiving for Your Incarnation as The Way, The Truth, and The Life.

MEDITATION ON OUR EUCHARISTIC LORD WHILE PRAYING THE "ANIMA CHRISTI"

✳ SOUL OF CHRIST, SANCTIFY ME ✳

Make me pure, my Jesus. Make me long for union with You in prayer more than anything else in this world. Make me spiritually beautiful so that all the people whose lives I touch will want what You give and will crave holiness. I want to carry You to Your people.

Remind me of the value of my little aches and pains so that I remember to offer them back to You for the salvation of souls. Make me ever grateful for every present You send me.

✳ BODY OF CHRIST, SAVE ME ✳

Dear Jesus, Your body was killed, brutally murdered, all for Your love. I keep trying to understand more fully how Your death was necessary for our salvation. It seems so senseless when thinking about it in human terms.

Nonetheless, I trust that I will find the salvation for which You gave Your life if I keep my sights on You. I can now receive You into my own body through the Blessed Sacrament. Please, dear Lord, lift the veil once in a while. Let me catch even just an occasional fleeting glimpse of awareness of what Your presence in the Eucharist is.

When I plead with You to forget my sins, remember how hard I tried to comprehend Your presence to me in the Eucharist. Remember how much I longed for the healing of Your Sacramental presence. Remember how I tried to love You, even though I fell hopelessly short.

✳ BLOOD OF CHRIST, INEBRIATE ME ✳

My sweet Jesus, Your precious Blood no longer flows onto the hard, dry earth, but I know Your wounds always bleed for love of us, for love of me. Thank You for suffering for me.

It is finished now. You won! You died for us and You won! Now I don't need to fear my sinfulness anymore. I can despise it and try to eradicate it, but fear is no longer the issue. Your mercy saves me. All I need to do is the best that I can, profess my sorrow at my failings, and You will wash me clean in Your Blood.

It is exciting, my Lord! You did all the dirty work, and I can reap the rewards. It isn't fair at all. How can I ever be grateful enough? How can I fail to love You and to trust You?

✳ WATER FROM THE SIDE OF CHRIST, WASH ME ✳

My very humanness, dear Jesus, makes me sinful. Although I know that You washed me clean of original sin in Baptism, I still have to take responsibility for my response to my own sinful nature. I am sorry for all my sins, dear Lord, and I beg You to continually wash away the guilt I carry.

Thank You, Jesus, for the wonderful Sacrament of Reconciliation. In it I can experience the actual washing clean of my soul which You accomplished for me on Calvary. The water flowing from Your side to cleanse me of my guilt is a shower of mercy I need all the time.

✳ PASSION OF CHRIST, STRENGTHEN ME ✳

Dear Jesus, You suffered so much to save me from the clutches of evil, and You are all powerful. By virtue of Your Passion, I beg You to be my force against evil.

I am weak, Lord, but I thank You for my weakness. If I had been mighty, I might not be as quick to realize how much I need Your strength. I want to depend on You. My little crosses are so much easier to bear when I have Your help to carry them. And Your help is what gives my crosses meaning and value; if You didn't help me carry them, they would be useless because they wouldn't be united with Your Passion.

✳ O GOOD JESUS, HEAR ME ✳

You never turn Your back on me, dear Lord. I have called, and You have answered. At the same time as I thank You for the mercy You've shown me, again, I beg You to hear the petitions I bring to You.

I ask for so much from You, sweet Jesus, but You are the only One who can give me what I seek. I trust in Your mercy and love, and my repetition of my requests isn't because I don't trust You, but rather because I don't trust myself to have always asked in the right way. I just did it again. I didn't trust that You would read my heart and know my needs. Dear Lord, more than anything, I need the presence of Your Spirit in my soul to increase my trust in You.

Will You accept the burden of my petitions, Lord? Will You watch over them while I burrow deeper and deeper into Your Sacred Heart? Please help me. Please read my heart and know what troubles me. Please grant me the peace of Your care.

✻ WITHIN THY WOUNDS, HIDE ME ✻

Sweet, precious Lord, the troubles of life in the world constantly keep my heart from being able to concentrate on You. Don't let me become so involved in earthly matters that I lose track of You.

I trust in the power of Your love, ever present in the wounds which always bleed for me. Shelter me from anything which keeps my heart from actively seeking You, my God.

✻ SUFFER ME NOT TO BE SEPARATED FROM THEE ✻

Jesus, when I forget Your will and follow my evil inclinations, please don't leave me floundering. Remember, I try to love You, even when I fail so miserably. You know my heart longs for You, even when I get distracted from You. I have to trust You to remember and not abandon me.

Wake me up to Your presence in my life when I lose sight of You and Your way. I couldn't go on living if I thought there was a chance You would let me go.

✻ FROM THE MALIGNANT ENEMY, DEFEND ME ✻

Dear Jesus, Satan is always present. He tries to take my heart away from its dedication to You.

My Lord, I am so little. I can't do it myself. I can't always stay free from the path of evil. I make mistakes. I sin. But I love You, and I don't want to lose You and the inheritance You won for me.

When temptations threaten my relationship with You, help me, Lord. Show me the way out. Show me the truth. Don't let me forget. Don't let me lose sight of You. You are all I have that I am guaranteed.

✳ IN THE HOUR OF MY DEATH, CALL ME AND BID ME COME TO THEE ✳

Jesus, be with me when I die. Lead me from this earthly body into the warmth of Your heavenly embrace. There, I will find safety and eternal love, peace and joy. When it is my time to go, please call to me so I will know which way to turn, so I will at last know with certainty that You are my home.

Meanwhile, I beg You, dear Lord, to keep me longing for You.

✳ THAT WITH THY SAINTS I MAY PRAISE THEE, FOREVER AND EVER ✳

What joy will be mine when I enter Heaven and see the Face of God! My Jesus, my trials will be over. The drudgeries of this earthly life will be past. I will claim the victory You won for me, not because I deserve it, but because of my trust in Your mercy.

Will there be anything then that can still the thrill of my soul? Will there be anything more I can long for than resting in peace, in total contentment, gazing on the One who loves me most and longest? Will anything be able to still my shouts of joy and praise to Him that gave me everything?

Thank You for offering me every opportunity to seek the gifts You promise.

✳ AMEN ✳

Jesus, I love You.

PART II
PRAYERS OF:

—Adoration

—Thanksgiving

—Petition

—Various Needs

PRAYERS OF ADORATION, THANKSGIVING, PETITIONS AND VARIOUS NEEDS

PRAISE

O Lord, You are my Lord and my God, yet I have never seen You.

You have created and redeemed me, and have conferred on me all my goods, yet I know You not.

I was created in order that I might know You, but I have not yet attained the goal of my creation. I confess, O Lord, and give You thanks, that You have created me in Your image, so that I might be mindful of You and contemplate You, and love You.

I seek not to understand in order that I may believe; rather, I believe in order that I may understand. Amen.

(Prayer of St. Anselm)

ACT OF CONSECRATION TO THE SACRED HEART OF JESUS

O Sacred Heart of Jesus, filled with infinite love, broken by my ingratitude, pierced by my sins, yet loving me still—accept the consecration that I make to You of all that I am and all that I have. Take every faculty of my soul and body. Draw me, day by day, nearer and nearer to your Sacred Heart, and there, as I can bear the lesson, teach me Your blessed ways. Amen.

ACT OF CONSECRATION TO THE IMMACULATE HEART OF MARY

Queen of the Most Holy Rosary, and tender Mother of all people, I consecrate myself to you and to your Immaculate Heart, and recommend to you my family, my country, and the whole human race.

Please accept my consecration, dearest Mother, and

use me as you wish, to accomplish your designs upon the world.

O Immaculate Heart of Mary, Queen of Heaven and Earth, rule over me, and teach me how to allow the heart of Jesus to rule and triumph in me and around me, as it has ruled and triumphed in you. Amen.

*(Pope Pius XII asked for the renewal of the Consecration to the Immaculate Heart of Mary, every year on May 31st—*ad coeli Reginam.)

CONSECRATION

Lord God, I know I am but a poor sinner; but I also believe in You, and Your love for me.

I believe that You offered me salvation through Your suffering and death.

My Lord, God, I may not have much to offer in return for this gift of life; but I offer all that I have.

I offer You my joys, my sufferings, my success, my failure.

I offer You my attempts, simply grant me persistence.

I offer You my pain, give me courage.

I offer You my talents, my accomplishments; they originated from you.

My Lord, God, I want You to be the first priority in my life, in my work, in my prayer, in my study, in my recreation, in my growth.

I offer You my life, but it is made worthy, only through Your grace. Amen.

ACT OF THANKSGIVING

From the depths of my heart I thank You, dear Lord, for Your infinite kindness in coming to me. How good You are to me! With Your most holy Mother and all the angels, I praise Your mercy and generosity toward me, a poor sinner. I thank You for nourishing my soul with Your Sacred Body and Precious Blood.

I will try to show my gratitude to You in the Sacrament of Your love, by obedience to Your holy commandments, by fidelity to my duties, by kindness to my neighbor and by an earnest endeavor to become more like You in my daily conduct.

Grant that I may spend the hours of the day gladly working with You according to Your will.

Help me just for today and be with me in it. In the long hours of work, that I may not grow weary or slack in serving You.

In conversations, that they may not be to me occasions of uncharitableness.

In the day's worries and disappointments, that I may be patient with myself and with those around me.

In moments of fatigue and illness, that I may be mindful of others rather than of myself.

In temptations, that I may be generous and loyal, so that when the day is over I may lay it at Your feet, with its successes which are all Yours, and its failures which are all my own, and feel that life is real and peaceful, and blessed when spent with You as the Guest of my soul. Amen.

Lord, I give thanks to You for Your dying on the Cross for my sins.

ADORATION

In the stillness, Lord, I adore You.

In the silence, I am with You.

Let my heart burn steadily as the flame which points to Your Presence, a light before men, a sign which calls to worship.

We have shared in Your Mysteries.

We have joyously offered the Sacrifice of our freedom and feasted on the reality of Your Body and Blood.

Our prayer, praise, and penance has been offered through You to the eternal Father, in the power of the Spirit.

Our feet have taken us from Your temple into the world, bearing You among men, bringing You into the midst of all for whom You died.

Now I return, Lord, to the still point where You abide always, taking forward in Your tabernacle the movements of our worship, enfolding in Your real Presence all our hopes and longings.

Lord, let me look forward to the celebration of the Mysteries. May these moments with You turn me towards the offering of Your Sacrifice and the feast of Your love.

(Rev. Peter Elliott)

THE ACT OF CHARITY

My God, because You are so good, I love You with all my heart, and for Your sake, I love my neighbor as myself.

If I love You, Lord, it is not because of Heaven which You have promised me.

If I fear to offend You, it is not because of Hell that threatens me.

What draws me to You, Lord, is Yourself alone. It is the sight of You, nailed to the Cross, Your body bruised in the pain of dying.

Your love so holds my heart, that if there were no Heaven, I would still love You. If there were no Hell, I would yet fear You.

I do not need Your gifts to make me love You, for even if I should have no hope at all of all the things I do hope for, I would still love You with the same love.

(St. Teresa of Avila)

PRAYER OF THE SEVEN GIFTS

Wisdom, come to me. In all my ways guide me, that mind and soul may be as one. Come, wise Spirit, come.

Understanding, enlighten me. Let this mind of mine, perceive deeply, comprehend and believe calmly. Come, understanding Spirit, come.

Counsel, whisper to me. Keep humble this creature asking for advice, for guidance in the problems of our lives. Come, counselling Spirit, come.

Knowledge, inform me. May I know the truths revealed, and know myself through truths of Faith. Come, knowing Spirit, come.

Strength, uphold me. Sustain this life, this breath, this soul, this flesh, and stand with me against the foe. Come, strong Spirit, come.

Devotion, raise me. My heart inflame with loving adoration, with praise and gratitude, with hope and joy. Come, devoted Spirit, come.

Fear of the Lord, penetrate me. With loving awe, let me come to You, in reverence for Your holiness, in wonder at Your Grace, on this alone may I depend. Come, awesome Spirit, come.

(Rev. Peter Elliott)

Come, Holy Spirit!
Breathe within me, Lord.
My Life, My Light.
Fire! Light! Truth!
Guide me, Holy Spirit.

MORNING PRAYER TO THE HOLY SPIRIT

Come, Holy Spirit, fill my heart with Your holy gifts.

Let my weakness be penetrated with Your strength this very day that I may fulfill all the duties of my state conscientiously, that I may do what is right and just.

Let my charity be such as to offend no one, and hurt no one's feelings; so generous as to pardon sincerely any wrong done to me.

Assist me, O Holy Spirit, in all my trials of life, enlighten me in my ignorance, advise me in my doubts, strengthen me in my weakness, help me in all my needs, protect me in temptations and console me in afflictions.

Graciously hear me, O Holy Spirit, and pour Your light into my heart, my soul, and my mind.

Assist me to live a holy life and to grow in goodness and grace. Amen.

(Secret of Sanctity)

PRAYER TO THE HOLY SPIRIT

Oh, Holy Spirit, beloved of my soul. . .I adore You. Enlighten me, guide me, strengthen me, console me. Tell me what I should do. . .give me Your orders. I promise to submit myself to all that You desire of me and to accept all that You permit to happen to me. Let me only know Your will.

(This submission to the Holy Spirit is the Secret of Sanctity—Cardinal Mercier.)

ACT OF ADORATION

Jesus, my God, I adore You, here present in the Blessed Sacrament of the altar, where You wait day and night to be our comfort while we await Your unveiled presence in heaven.

Jesus, my God, I adore You in all places where the Blessed Sacrament is reserved, in reparation for sins committed against this Sacrament of Love. Jesus, my God, I adore You for all time, past, present and future, for every soul that ever was, is or shall be created. Jesus, my God, who for us has endured hunger and cold, labor and fatigue, I adore You. Jesus, my God, who for my sake has deigned to subject Yourself to the humiliation of temptation, to the perfidy and defection of friends, to the scorn of Your enemies, I adore You.

Jesus, my God, who for us has endured the buffeting of Your passion, the scourging, the crowning with thorns, the heavy weight of the Cross, I adore You. Jesus, my God, who, for my salvation and that of all mankind, was cruelly nailed to the Cross and hung there for three long hours in bitter agony, I adore You.

Jesus, my God, who for love of us did institute this Blessed Sacrament and offer Yourself daily for the sins of men, I adore You. Jesus, my God, who in Holy Communion became the food of my soul, I adore You.

Jesus, for You I live. Jesus, for You I die. Jesus, I am Yours in life and death.

(John J. Cardinal Carberry)

PRAYER OF THANKSGIVING

I thank You, Jesus:

For the gift of life, and every moment I live! For my health, even though at times I may have been ill, or suffered serious reverses and sufferings. So often these and other crosses are blessings in disguise. For the world about me, such as, the glories of nature, the moon, the stars, the flowers of the fields, the fruits of the earth, the very air I breathe, the refreshing rains, the glorious sunshine, the seasons of the year. For my parents, my relatives, my treasured and trusted friends.

I thank You:

For the gift of my faith. For the gift of Yourself in the Incarnation in which You became man, lived for me, taught me by Your word and example. For the gift of redemption, which You accomplished by Your sufferings, death and resurrection—all this for my salvation.

O my God, I thank You for all the favors You have bestowed upon me. I give You thanks from the bottom of my heart for having created me, and for all the joys of life, and its sorrows, too, for the home You gave me, for the loved ones with which You have surrounded me, for the friends I have made through life.

My Lord, I thank You for guarding me always and keeping me safe; I thank You for giving me so often in the sacrament of Penance forgiveness for my sins; for offering Yourself in Holy Mass with all Your infinite merits to the Father for me; for coming to me in Holy Communion, in spite of the coldness of my welcome; for the patient waiting in the adorable sacrament of the altar.

My Jesus, I thank You for having lived, suffered, and died for me. I thank You for Your love. I thank You, Lord, for preparing a place for me in heaven where I hope to be happy with You, and to thank You for all eternity. Amen.

John J. Cardinal Carberry, Archbishop of St. Louis
December 8, 1977

PRAYER BEFORE A CRUCIFIX

Look down upon me, O Good and Gentle Jesus, while before Your face I humbly kneel, and with the most fervent desire of my soul, I pray and beseech You to fix deep in my heart lively sentiments of faith, hope and charity, true contrition for my sins, and a firm purpose of amendment; while with deep affection and grief of soul I mentally contemplate Your five most precious wounds, recalling to mind the words which David, Your prophet, said concerning You: *They have pierced My hands and My feet, they have numbered all My bones.*

FOR HEALING

Lord, You came that Your people might have life, and have it to the fullest. Your ministry was dedicated to it. You healed so many, showed so much compassion for those in need. There is so much healing needed now, Lord.

As I pray for healing, I offer You my faith, as those did who sought You out while You were on earth. The woman said she needed only to touch Your cloak. The lepers came in faith. The blind man asked, "that I might see, Lord." Martha and Mary said that had You been present, Lazarus would not have died. So You brought him back to life, Lord. The Centurion admitted that You didn't even have to return to his home with him to heal; You need only to will it so. How many have You healed, Lord? Physically, emotionally, spiritually?

Divine Physician, I come to You now to ask for healing for ___(specify)___. I bring You this need knowing only You alone have such power. Trusting in Your mercy and compassion, Lord, I place all in Your hands. If it be Your will deliver Your servant from this affliction.

Lord Jesus, may Your healing love be an obvious reflection of Your power and majesty. May it be attributable to You alone and for Your greater honor and glory. May it be a conversion for sinners, a hope for those in need, a beacon of light for those lost. Jesus, I trust in You. Heal, Lord Jesus!

RECONCILIATION

The Prayer of the Penitent (Act of Contrition)

O my God, I am very sorry that I have sinned against you. You are my Saviour and Lord. Through Your grace, help me to not sin again.

* * *

Loving Father, in repentance I come to You acknowledging my sins, and recognize I no longer deserve to be called Your child. Have mercy on me.

Lord Jesus, You came into the world to save sinners, to draw all unto Yourself. Through Your death and resurrection save me from all my sins, that I might seek Your will and find the peace You offer to mankind.

Holy Spirit, source of all gifts, I cry out to You with confidence and ask that You teach me to live as a child of light.

Saviour of the world, You forgave from Your cross. Along with the good thief, I ask You, "Lord, remember me when You come into Your kingdom."

HEALING PRAYER AT BEDTIME

Jesus, through the power of the Holy Spirit, go back into my memory as I sleep. Every hurt that has ever been done to me—heal that hurt. Every hurt that I have caused to another person—heal that hurt. All the relationships that have been damaged in my whole life that I am not aware of—heal those relationships.

But Lord, if there is anything that I need to do—if I need to go to a person because he is still suffering from my hand, bring to my awareness that person.

I choose to forgive and I ask to be forgiven. Remove whatever bitterness may be in my heart, Lord, and fill the empty spaces with Your Love.

Thank You, Jesus. Amen.

FOR HOLY CHURCH AND FOR PRIESTS

O my Jesus, I beg You on behalf of the whole Church: Grant it love and the light of Your Spirit and give power to the words of priests so that hardened hearts might be brought to repentance and return to You, O Lord.

Lord, give us holy priests; You yourself maintain them in holiness. O Divine and Great High Priest, may the power of Your mercy accompany them everywhere and protect them from the devil's traps and snares which are continually being set for the souls of priests. May the power of Your mercy, O Lord, shatter and bring to naught all that might tarnish the sanctity of priests, for You can do all things. I ask You, Jesus, for a special blessing and for light for the priests before whom I will make my confessions throughout my lifetime. Amen.

PRAYER FOR VOCATIONS

Lord, You told us that "The harvest indeed is great but the laborers are few. Pray, therefore, the Lord of the harvest to send laborers into His fields." We ask You to strengthen us as we follow the vocation to which You have called us. We pray particularly for those called to serve as priests, sisters, brothers and deacons:

Those whom You have called,
Those You are calling now,
Those You will call in the future.

May they be open and responsive to the call of serving Your people. We ask this through Christ, our Lord, Amen.

PRAYER FOR THE POPE

Lord, source of eternal life and truth, give to Your shepherd, the Pope, a spirit of courage and right judgment, a spirit of knowledge and love.

By governing with fidelity those entrusted to his care may he, as successor to the apostle Peter and vicar of Christ, build Your Church into a sacrament of unity, love, and peace for all the world.

We ask this through our Lord Jesus Christ, Your Son, Who lives and reigns with You and the Holy Spirit, one God, forever and ever. Amen.

PRAYER TO ST. JOSEPH FOR A HAPPY DEATH

O Powerful, St. Joseph, great patron of the dying, you who breathed your last in the arms of Jesus and Mary, I implore you to stand by me at the hour of my death. Remember at that time, how often I have called upon you. Obtain for me perfect contrition for my sins, firm confidence in the mercy of God, firm trust in the merits of my Saviour and the grace to breathe forth my soul while sweetly calling upon the holy names, Jesus, Mary and Joseph. Obtain this favor for me through your Divine Foster Son, Jesus Christ, Who with the Father and the Holy Spirit lives and reigns forever and ever. Amen.

Jesus, Mary and Joseph, I give you my heart and my soul!

Jesus, Mary and Joseph, assist me in my last agony.

Jesus, Mary and Joseph, may I breathe forth my soul at peace in your blessed company!

PRAYER FOR THE POOR SOULS
(Taught to St. Gertrude)

(Our Lord told St. Gertrude the Great that the following prayer would release a vast number of souls from Purgatory each time it is said.)

Eternal Father, I offer Thee the most Precious Blood of Thy Divine Son, Jesus, in union with all the Masses being said this day throughout the world for all the holy souls in Purgatory. Amen.

(Approval of His Emminence the Cardinal Patriarch of Lisbon—4/3/1936.)

PRAYER FOR THE DYING

Most Merciful Jesus, lover of souls, I pray You, by the agony of Your most Sacred Heart, and by the sorrows of Your Immaculate Mother, to wash in Your Most Precious Blood, the sinners of the world who are now in their agony, and who will die today.

Heart of Jesus, once in agony, have mercy on the dying. Amen.

FOR THE GIFT OF LIFE

My God, creator of all that exists, I offer praise for the wonder of Your creation, thanksgiving for the gift of life, and beg Your mercy for our misuse of Your gifts. I affirm there is no greater gift than life itself, mankind created unto Your image and likeness; souls brought forth with the invitation to share the glories of Heaven with You.

My God, I pray for all life You have created. Even the plants, the trees, the grass, the birds, the animals, the life in the seas, are all the work of Your hand. But mostly I pray for human life and I thank You for all the souls You have created, each gender, each race, each color; for the rich and poor, the strong and weak.

My God, I pray for the needs of all of the souls you create; for their salvation and for their material needs.

My God, I pray especially for the children, so often neglected or abused. I pray for all parents that they might guide and direct their children, and entrust them to Your love and protection.

My God, I pray for the gift of life you have placed into our hands, the power to reproduce the human race, to bring new souls into the world.

My God, I most ardently pray for forgiveness, imploring Your compassion for our misuse of that power. I pray for all the aborted infants that have been denied the gift of life. Have them all with You, my God. I pray for their parents, that they might find peace and forgiveness for their actions. I pray for all those who support, assist, or perform that act that takes a human life.

My God, I pray for all those who have participated in any way in the horrors of violence and persecution, for the destruction of war. I pray for myself, and for all of mankind who, through our sins, caused the crucifixion of Your Son, our Saviour, Jesus Christ.

PARENTS PRAYER TO THE HOLY FAMILY

Jesus, Son of the Eternal Father, we most fervently implore You to take our children under Your special care and enclose them in the love of Your Sacred Heart. Rule and guide them that they may live according to our holy Faith, that they may not waiver in their confidence in You, and may ever remain faithful in Your love.

O Mary, blessed Mother of Jesus, grant to our children a place in your pure maternal heart. Spread over them your protecting mantle when danger threatens their innocence; keep them firm when they are tempted to stray from the path of virtue; and should they have the misfortune to fall, oh, raise them up again and reconcile them with your Divine Son.

Holy foster father, St. Joseph, watch over our children. Protect them from the assaults of the wicked enemy, and deliver them from all dangers of soul and body.

Mary and Joseph, dear parents of the holy Child Jesus, intercede for us that we may be a good example and bring up our children in the love and fear of God, and one day attain with them the Beatific Vision in Heaven. Amen.

PRAYER FOR A FAMILY

O dear Jesus, I humbly implore You to grant Your special graces to our family. May our home be the shrine of peace, purity, love, labor and faith. I beg You, dear Jesus, to protect and bless all of us, absent and present, living and dead.

O Mary, loving Mother of Jesus, and our Mother, pray to Jesus for our family, for all the families of the world, to guard the cradle of the newborn, the schools of the young and their vocations.

Blessed Saint Joseph, holy guardian of Jesus and Mary, assist us by your prayers in all the necessities of life. Ask of Jesus that special grace which He granted to you, to watch over our home at the pillow of the sick and the dying, so that with Mary and with you, heaven may find our family unbroken in the Sacred Heart of Jesus. Amen.

PRAYER OF SPOUSES FOR EACH OTHER

Lord Jesus, grant that I and my spouse may have a true and understanding love for each other. Grant that we may both be filled with faith and trust. Give us the grace to live with each other in peace and harmony. May we always bear with one another's weaknesses and grow from each other's strengths.

Help us to forgive one another's failings and grant us patience, kindness, cheerfulness and the spirit of placing the well-being of one another ahead of self.

May the love that brought us together grow and mature with each passing year. Bring us both ever closer to You through our love for each other. Let our love grow to perfection. Amen.

LEARNING CHRIST

Teach me, my Lord, to be sweet and gentle in all the events of life, in disappointments, in the thoughtlessness of those I trusted, in the unfaithfulness of those on whom I relied. Let me put myself aside, to think of the happiness of others, to hide my little pains and heartaches, so that I may be the only one to suffer from them. Teach me to profit by the suffering that comes across my path. Let me so use it that it may mellow me, not harden nor embitter me; that it may make me patient, not irritable. That it may make me broad in my forgiveness, not narrow, haughty and overbearing. May no one be less good for having come within my influence. No one less pure, less true, less kind, less noble for having been a fellow-traveler in our journey toward Eternal Life. As I go my rounds from one distraction to another, let me whisper from time to time, a word of love to Thee. May my life be lived in the supernatural, full of power for good, and strong in its purpose of sanctity. Amen.

CHANGE US LORD

Dear Jesus, please help us to change. Guide us to Your eternal wisdom so that whatever we do is for Your honor and glory. Make our advancement suit Your desires for us. As You are unchanging, change us to be the people You created us to be.

Show us Your expectations. We keep forgetting and becoming distracted. We are spiritual babies, crawling toward You, but we become mesmerized by the lights, bells and whistles placed around us. When we tarry, Lord, point us back in the right direction. When we become enthralled with all that we are, remind us of who You are. Direct us always into Your loving embrace.

We have so much, dear Jesus, but we have nothing when we don't have You. Startle us, if You must, with the light of Your truth. Jar us from the glitter and glamour into the harsh reality of our personal responsibilities. Lead us to options for the poor, ethical standards and practices, respect for life. Help us to see that less is more. Show us the wealth of fewer earthly pleasures and more spiritual pleasures. Draw us to You, dear Jesus. Don't let us become distracted from You.

MY TRUE NEEDS

Lord, You told us: *All that you ask of the Father in my name will be given unto you.* You asked us to ask. But, maybe there's a catch to that. Maybe you mean that You will give us what we TRULY need, instead of what we want. Do people usually ask for what they want without truly recognizing what they really need? Maybe I need to formulate my needs more attuned to my place in eternity.

First of all, I need You. I need a true and deep relationship with You, Lord, because without it, nothing else is ever going to work, or at least it won't last. I need food for my soul. I need to recognize the need for daily prayer in my life and a zest for it. I need to find the true meaning of the Mass, and to be able to go there with purpose, to really get into what is happening there.

Lord, I need to put deeper meaning into my everyday life as well. It seems like there could be so much more depth to my job, my marriage, my family. It just shouldn't all be taken for granted as much as it is, from day to day. I could do so much more with my daily life. But, I need Your grace to do it.

Would there be greater accomplishment in my life if I were more compassionate, more sharing, more dependent on You and what You want me to be, or to achieve? Should I be giving You more control of my life?

Jesus! I bring You my package of needs. You asked us to. Funny thing, money and success weren't included. Peace, happiness, and faith are. Jesus, I've just realized money and success can't buy those. You give them to us.

IN THANKS, LORD

Dear, sweet Jesus, even as I thank You, I ask for more. Shower me with Your graces, Lord, that I will always praise You for Your gifts to me. Never let me forget Who is the Giver and who is the receiver. Let my life be a testimony of Your generosity to all who call on You.

Dear Lord, please touch the hearts of those who neither know how to be grateful nor even know to ask for Your gifts. Help us all to find the wonders You eagerly offer us. Help us to recognize the joy in embracing the sorrow. Help us to discover the healing balm You offer in the pain. Help us to know Your power in Your quiet humility and love.

Thank You, Lord, for allowing me to recognize and accept so many of Your gifts. I love You, Jesus. Thank You for Your love.

THANKSGIVING

I asked God for strength,
that I might achieve...

I was made weak,
that I might learn humbly to obey.

I asked for health,
that I might do greater things...

I was given infirmity,
that I might do better things...

I asked for riches,
that I might be happy...

I was given poverty,
that I might be wise.

I asked for power,
that I might have the praise of men...

I was given weakness,
that I might feel the need of God.

I asked for all things,
that I might enjoy life...

I was given life,
that I might enjoy all things.

I got nothing that I asked for,
but everything I had hoped for.

Almost despite myself,
my unspoken prayers were answered.

I am among all mankind, most richly blessed!

THE SALVE REGINA

Hail, Holy Queen, Mother of Mercy.

Our life, our sweetness and our hope!

To you do we cry, poor banished children of Eve.

To you do we send up our sighs; mourning and weeping in this vale of tears.

Turn then, most gracious Advocate, your eyes of mercy toward us; and after this, our exile, show unto us the blessed fruit of your womb, Jesus.

O clement, O loving, O sweet Virgin Mary.

Pray for us, O holy Mother of God. That we may be made worthy of the promises of Christ.

PRAYERS TAUGHT TO THE CHILDREN AT FATIMA (1917)

PARDON PRAYER

(Taught by the Angel)

O My God, I believe, I adore, I trust and I love You! And I beg pardon for those who do not believe, do not adore, do not trust, and do not love You.

PRAYER OF REPARATION

(With the Blessed Sacrament suspended in the air, the Angel at Fatima prostrated himself and recited this prayer.)

O Most Holy Trinity, Father, Son and Holy Spirit, I adore You profoundly. I offer You the most precious Body, Blood, Soul and Divinity of Jesus Christ, present in all the tabernacles of the world, in reparation for the outrages, sacrileges and indifference by which He is offended. By the infinite merits of the Sacred Heart of Jesus and the Immaculate Heart of Mary, I beg the conversion of poor sinners.

EUCHARISTIC PRAYER

Most Holy Trinity, I adore You! My God, my God, I love You in the Most Blessed Sacrament!

SACRIFICE PRAYER

(To be said in offering to Our Lord our pains and hurts, both physically and mentally, in reparation.)

O my Jesus, it is for love of You, in reparation for the offenses committed against the Immaculate Heart of Mary, and for the conversion of poor sinners.

ROSARY DECADE PRAYER

(To be said at the end of each decade of the Rosary.)

O my Jesus, forgive us our sins, save us from the fires of hell. Lead all souls to Heaven, especially those most in need of Your mercy.

A PRAYER FOR DIVINE MERCY

O Great Merciful God, Infinite Goodness, today all mankind calls out from the abyss of its misery to Your mercy—to Your compassion, O God; and it is with its mighty voice of misery that it cries out. Gracious God, do not reject the prayer of this earth's exiles! O Lord, Goodness beyond our understanding, Who are acquainted with our misery through and through, and know that by our own power we cannot ascend to You, we implore You, anticipate us with Your grace and keep on increasing Your mercy in us, that we may faithfully do Your holy will all through our life and at death's hour. Let the omnipotence of Your mercy shield us from the darts of our salvation's enemies, that we may with confidence, as Your children, await Your final coming—that day known to You alone. And we expect to obtain everything promised us by Jesus in spite of all our wretchedness, for Jesus is our Hope. Through His merciful Heart, as through an open gate, we pass through to heaven.

(From the Diary of the Servant of God, by Sr. Faustina)
Imprimatur: J. F. Maguire, Bishop of Springfield, MA. Nov. 13, 1979.

PRAYER FOR PEACE

O God, from Whom proceeds all holy desires, all right counsels and all just works; grant unto us Your servants that peace which the world cannot give. May our hearts be devoted to Your service, and that, being delivered from the fear of our enemies, we may pass our time in peace under Your protection. Through Christ Our Lord, Amen.

THE WAY OF THE CROSS

(From the Passionist Fathers)

PRAYER

Crucified Jesus, behold me at Your feet. I ask Your pardon for having wandered so often into the bypaths of sin. In making this Way of the Cross give me courage to follow faithfully in Your blood-stained path.

I STATION: *Jesus Is Condemned To Death*

Our innocent Saviour accepts the unjust sentence of death on the Cross to atone for my sins.

Petition: Divine Jesus, help me to accept the injustices of life in reparation for my many sins.

Our Father...

II STATION: *Jesus Carries His Cross*

The burden of the Cross demanded heroic sacrifice from our Blessed Lord, yet, willingly He accepts it for love of us.

Petition: O Lord, give me the courage to take up my Cross daily and to carry it patiently along life's way.

Our Father...

III STATION: *Jesus Falls The First Time*

The heavy Cross and the weight of man's sinfulness overwhelm the Divine Victim and He falls into the dust of the street.

Petition: My Jesus, when the sorrows of life overwhelm me, help me to rise above human weakness.

Our Father...

IV STATION: ***Jesus Meets His Mother***

The heart of Mary was pierced with sorrow, when she saw her innocent Son carrying the Cross made so heavy by my sins.

Petition: Suffering Lord, impress on me how much I need the consolation and help of Your sorrowful Mother.

Our Father...

V STATION: ***Simon Of Cyrene Helps Jesus Carry The Cross***

Our blessed Lord was so weak and tired that He permitted Simon to help Him carry the Cross.

Petition: Without Your help, O Jesus, I can never carry my cross in life alone.

Our Father...

VI STATION: ***Veronica Wipes The Face Of Jesus***

The image of the Saviour was imprinted on the veil which the compassionate Veronica pressed to the face of Jesus.

Petition: Suffering Master, may I often think of You, that the loving memory of Your sufferings be imprinted on my heart.

Our Father...

VII STATION: ***The Second Fall Of Jesus***

Because of agonizing pain and weakness, Jesus falls once more, but rising again, carries the Cross onward.

Petition: O Lord, by this fall strengthen me against discouragement, and help me never to stop loving and serving You.

Our Father...

VIII STATION: ***Jesus Consoles The Women Of Jerusalem***

Jesus forgets His own sorrow and pain to console the weeping women of Jerusalem.

Petition: Blessed Saviour, in sorrows and afflictions assist me to forget myself and to help others.

Our Father...

IX STATION: ***The Third Fall Of Jesus***

On the slopes of Calvary Jesus falls the third time, yet He struggles to His feet, determined to reach the place of sacrifice.

Petition: O Divine Master, give me courage to persevere in leading a good life and reaching Heaven.

Our Father...

X STATION: ***Jesus Is Stripped Of His Garments***

The blood-soaked garments are torn from the scourged body of Jesus, so He might die stripped of every comfort in life.

Petition: Agonizing Jesus, strip me of all intemperance in the use of life's comfort and pleasures.

Our Father...

XI STATION: ***Jesus Is Nailed To The Cross***

How frightful the agony of Jesus as the soldiers hammer rough nails through His hands and feet.

Petition: Crucified Saviour, You forgave Your enemies, teach me to also forgive injuries and to forget them.

Our Father...

XII STATION: ***Jesus Dies On The Cross***

The Divine Victim, obedient unto death, gives the supreme proof of His love for men.

Petition: My Jesus, help me to make my return of love by life-long obedience to Your commandments.

Our Father...

XIII STATION: ***Jesus Is Taken Down From The Cross***

What grief and tragedy as Mary holds to her broken heart, the lifeless body of Her Son.

Petition: O Mother of Sorrows, keep close to me during life and especially at the hour of my death.
Our Father...

XIV STATION: ***Jesus Is Laid In The Sepulcher***

The Body of Jesus was reverently laid in the tomb by His loving Mother and devoted disciples.

Petition: Dear Mother Mary, help me to make my heart a fit resting place for the Body of Jesus, when I receive Him in Holy Communion.

PRAYERS FROM THE SAINTS

To Mary

O Mary, powerful Virgin, you are the mighty and glorious protector of the Church; you are the marvelous help of Christians; you are powerful as an army set in battle array; you alone have destroyed every heresy in the whole world.

In the midst of our anguish, our struggles and our distress, defend us from the power of the enemy and at the hour of our death receive our souls in paradise. Amen. (St. John Bosco)

God's Will

Lord, grant that I may always allow myself to be guided by You, always follow Your plans and perfectly accomplish Your holy will.

Grant that in all things, great and small, today and all the days of my life, I may do whatever You require of me. Help me respond to the slightest prompting of Your grace so that I may be Your trustworthy instrument for Your honor.

May Your will be done in time and in eternity—by me, in me and through me. Amen. (St. Teresa of Avila)

God's Will

Dearest Lord, teach me to be generous; teach me to serve You as You deserve; to give and not to count the cost, to fight and not to heed the wounds, to toil and not to seek for rest, to labor and not to ask for reward except that of knowing I am doing Your will.

(St. Ignatius Loyola)

Peace Prayer

Lord, make me an instrument of Thy peace; where there is hatred, let me sow love; where there is injury, pardon; where there is doubt, faith; where there is despair, hope; where there is darkness, light; and where there is sadness, joy.

O Divine Master, grant that I may not so much seek to be consoled as to console; to be understood as to understand; to be loved, as to love; for it is in giving that we receive, it is in pardoning that we are pardoned, and it is in dying that we are born to eternal life.

(St. Francis of Assisi)

PART III

PREPARED FORMAT FOR ONE HOUR OF ADORATION

1. ROSARY (THE SORROWFUL MYSTERIES)	(15 to 20 min.)
2. PRAYERS OR MEDITATIONS	(10 to 15 min.)
3. CHAPLET OF DIVINE MERCY and DIVINE MERCY PRAYER	(10 min.)
4. LITANY OF THE SACRED HEART	(8 min.)
5. PRAYERS AND MEDITATIONS	(12 min.)

VARIOUS MEDITATIONS AVAILABLE IN THIS BOOK:
Part I, page 3.

VARIOUS PRAYERS AVAILABLE IN THIS BOOK:
Part II, page 43.

HOW TO SAY THE ROSARY

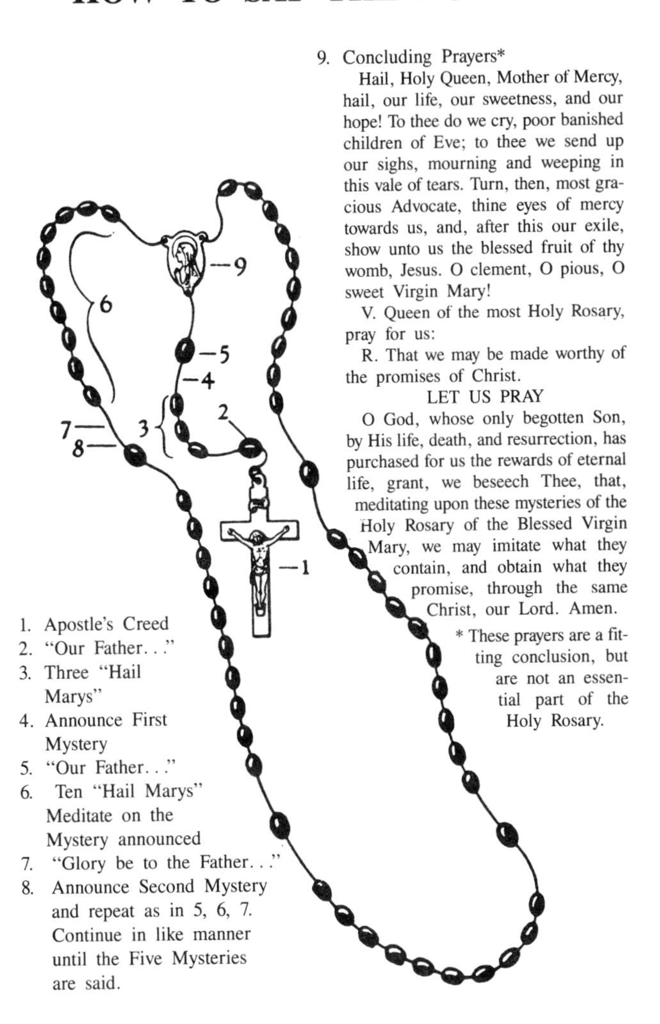

9. Concluding Prayers*

Hail, Holy Queen, Mother of Mercy, hail, our life, our sweetness, and our hope! To thee do we cry, poor banished children of Eve; to thee we send up our sighs, mourning and weeping in this vale of tears. Turn, then, most gracious Advocate, thine eyes of mercy towards us, and, after this our exile, show unto us the blessed fruit of thy womb, Jesus. O clement, O pious, O sweet Virgin Mary!

V. Queen of the most Holy Rosary, pray for us:

R. That we may be made worthy of the promises of Christ.

LET US PRAY

O God, whose only begotten Son, by His life, death, and resurrection, has purchased for us the rewards of eternal life, grant, we beseech Thee, that, meditating upon these mysteries of the Holy Rosary of the Blessed Virgin Mary, we may imitate what they contain, and obtain what they promise, through the same Christ, our Lord. Amen.

* These prayers are a fitting conclusion, but are not an essential part of the Holy Rosary.

1. Apostle's Creed
2. "Our Father. . ."
3. Three "Hail Marys"
4. Announce First Mystery
5. "Our Father. . ."
6. Ten "Hail Marys" Meditate on the Mystery announced
7. "Glory be to the Father. . ."
8. Announce Second Mystery and repeat as in 5, 6, 7. Continue in like manner until the Five Mysteries are said.

THE SCRIPTURAL ROSARY

The Scriptural Rosary combines the regular recitation of the rosary, with passages from scripture, said before each **Hail Mary**. The scripture passages evolve so that the story of each mystery, or decade, unfolds on a bead by bead basis. The passages also tie into the meditation given before the decade. It is a great aid for meditating on the mysteries.

Each decade is composed of the standard: **Our Father,** ten **Hail Marys** and the **Glory Be.** The decade finishes with the Fatima prayer, *O my Jesus, forgive us our sins, save us from the fires of hell and lead all souls to heaven, especially those in most need of Your mercy.*

A meditation and a prayer intention begins each decade.

PRAYERS OF THE ROSARY

The Apostle's Creed

I believe in God, the Father Almighty, Creator of heaven and earth; and in Jesus Christ, His only Son, our Lord; Who was conceived by the Holy Spirit, born of the Virgin Mary, suffered under Pontius Pilate, was crucified, died and was buried. He descended to the dead, the third day He rose again. He ascended into heaven, sits at the right hand of God, the Father Almighty; from thence He shall come to judge the living and the dead. I believe in the Holy Spirit, the holy Catholic Church, the communion of Saints, the forgiveness of sins, the resurrection of the body, and life everlasting. Amen.

Our Father

Our Father, Who art in heaven, hallowed be Thy name; Thy Kingdom come; Thy will be done, on earth, as it is in heaven. Give us this day our daily bread; and forgive us our trespasses, as we forgive those who trespass against us; and lead us not into temptation, but deliver us from evil. Amen.

Hail Mary

Hail Mary, full of grace; the Lord is with thee; blessed art thou among women, and blessed is the fruit of thy womb, Jesus. Holy Mary, Mother of God, pray for us sinners, now and at the hour of our death. Amen.

Glory be to the Father

Glory be to the Father, and to the Son, and to the Holy Spirit, As it was in the beginning, is now, and ever shall be, world without end. Amen.

THE SORROWFUL MYSTERIES

1. THE AGONY IN THE GARDEN

Jesus prayed with great intensity and anguish over His impending death. His agony, perhaps, was an inner one; a distress and sadness that the death He was about to undergo, would be suffered in vain for many. Like Jesus, we also face crucial decisions, stress and difficulty, and pain in our daily lives. If we can kneel with Jesus in His agony, He will be there in ours.

Prayer Intention

Let us pray for all those who suffer, physically, and emotionally; all those who are spiritually ill. Let us pray that their agony can be united with that of Jesus, and not lost through despair or resentment.

Our Father...

1. Then Jesus went with them to a place called Gethsemani; and He began to experience sorrow and distress. (*Mt.* 26:36-37)—**Hail Mary...**
2. Then He said to them, *My heart is nearly broken with sorrow. Remain here and stay awake with Me.* (*Mt.* 26:38)—**Hail Mary...**
3. He withdrew from them and knelt down and prayed. (*Lk.* 22:41)—**Hail Mary...**
4. *Father, if it is possible, let this cup pass from me. Still, let it be as you would have it, not as I.* (*Mt.* 26:39)—**Hail Mary...**
5. When He returned to His disciples, He found them asleep. He said to Peter, *So you could not stay awake*

with me for even an hour? Be on guard and pray that you may not undergo the test. The spirit is willing, but nature is weak. (*Mt.* 26:40-42)—**Hail Mary...**

6. In His anguish, He prayed more earnestly. An angel appeared to Him, coming from Heaven to give Him strength. (*Lk.* 22:44-43)—**Hail Mary...**

7. *The hour is on us when the Son of Man is to be handed over to the power of evil men.* (*Mt.* 26:45)—**Hail Mary...**

8. While He was still speaking, Judas, one of the twelve, arrived accompanied by a great crowd with swords and clubs. (*Mt.* 26, 47)—**Hail Mary...**

9. He immediately went over to Jesus, said to Him, *Peace, Rabbi,* and embraced Him. (*Mt.* 26:49)—**Hail Mary...**

10. Jesus answered, *Friend, do what you are here for.* At that moment they stepped forward to lay hands on Jesus and arrested Him. (*Mt.* 26:50)—**Hail Mary...**

Glory be to the Father...
O My Jesus, forgive us our sins...

2. THE SCOURGING AT THE PILLAR

Pilate, disturbed at the meek majesty of his prisoner, had Him scourged at the pillar, though he could not find any fault in Him. Perhaps he simply resented the fact that Jesus had no use for this world, Pilate's world, and spoke so overwhelmingly for the next world. Which way do we view this world? Can we offer and accept our suffering as a sacrifice to God, as Jesus offered His life for us?

Prayer Intention

Let us offer this decade in thanksgiving for the sacrifices made by Our Lord for the love of us. Pray also, in reparation for all the sins of the world inflicted upon the Sacred Heart of Jesus, and the indifference to His Mother.

Our Father...

1. As soon as it was daybreak, the chief priests, with the elders and scribes, reached a decision. They bound Jesus, led Him away, and handed Him over to Pilate. Pilate interrogated Him, *Are you the King of the Jews*? (*Mk.* 15:1-2)—**Hail Mary...**
2. Jesus answered, *My Kingdom does not belong to this world.* At this pilate said to Him, *So then you are a King?* Jesus replied, *It is you who say I am a King. The reason I was born, the reason why I came into the world is to testify to the truth. Anyone committed to the truth, hears my voice.* (*John* 18:36-37)—**Hail Mary...**
3. *This much only will I say, From now on, the Son of Man will have his seat at the right hand of the Power of God.* (*Lk.* 22:69)—**Hail Mary...**
4. *So you are the Son of God?* they asked in chorus. He answered, *It is you who say that I am.* (*Lk.* 22:70)—**Hail Mary...**
5. Pilate's next move was to take Jesus and have Him scourged. (*John* 19:1)—**Hail Mary...**
6. Despised and rejected by men, a man of sorrows. (*Is.* 53:3)—**Hail Mary...**
7. And yet, ours were the sufferings He bore. (*Is.* 53:4)—**Hail Mary...**
8. He was pierced through for our faults, crushed for our sins. (*Is.* 53:5)—**Hail Mary...**
9. They blindfolded Him, slapped Him and then taunted Him. (*Lk.* 23:64)—**Hail Mary...**

10. And after He had Jesus scourged, Pilate handed Him over to be crucified. (*Mk.* 15:15)—**Hail Mary...**

Glory be to the Father...
O My Jesus, forgive us our sins...

3. THE CROWNING OF THORNS

The coronation, offered to Jesus by the world, was a crown of thorns. How do we crown Him now? Do we deny Him, or simply show indifference? Do we truly seek Him out?

Prayer Intention

Let us offer this decade for all people who suffer under oppression and persecution. Those who suffer humiliation and rejection. And we pray in reparation to God for the sins of the world, the thorns of the crown.

Our Father...

1. The soldiers now led Jesus away into the hall known as the Praetorium; at the time they assembled the whole cohort. (*Mk.* 15:16)—**Hail Mary...**

2. They dressed Him in royal purple, then wove a crown of thorns and put it on Him. (*Mk.* 15:17)—**Hail Mary...**

3. They began to salute Him, *All hail! King of the Jews!* (*Mk.* 15:18)—**Hail Mary...**

4. Continually striking Jesus on the head with a reed and spitting at Him, they genuflected before Him and pretended to pay Him homage. (*Mk.* 15:19)—**Hail Mary...**

5. Pilate said to the crowd: *Observe what I do. I am going to bring Him out to you to make you realize that I find no case against Him.* (*John* 19:4)—**Hail Mary...**

6. When Jesus came out wearing the crown of thorns and the purple cloak, Pilate said to them, *Look at the Man!* (*John* 19:5)—**Hail Mary...**
7. As soon as the chief priests and the temple guards saw Him they shouted, *Crucify Him! Crucify Him!* (*Jn.* 19:6)—**Hail Mary...**
8. *Why, what crime has He committed?* asked Pilate. They only shouted the louder, *Crucify Him!* (*Mk.* 15:14)—**Hail Mary...**
9. Pilate said to the Jews, *Look at your King.* (*Jn.* 19:14)—**Hail Mary...**
10. In the end, Pilate handed Jesus over to be crucified. (*Jn.* 19:16)—**Hail Mary...**

Glory be to the Father...
O My Jesus, forgive us our sins...

4. THE CARRYING OF THE CROSS

The Son of God carries the instrument of His death to the hill of Calvary. Jesus' carrying of the cross was a fulfillment of His earlier words, *Let all who would believe in me, take up their cross and follow me.* A cross He didn't have to carry. Neither do we, unless we choose Jesus over Satan and sin.

Prayer Intention

Let us pray for the suffering, the lonely, the homeless. Let us ask Jesus to give special meaning to the crosses they carry.

Our Father...

1. When they had finished making a fool of Him, they stripped Jesus of the cloak, dressed Him in His own clothes, and led Him off to crucifixion. (*Mt.* 27:31)—**Hail Mary...**

2. On their way out they met a Cyrenian named Simon. This man they pressed into service to carry the cross. (*Mt.* 27:32)—**Hail Mary...**
3. A great crowd of people followed Him, including women who beat their breasts and lamented over Him. (*Lk.* 23:27)—**Hail Mary...**
4. Jesus turned to them and said: *Daughters of Jerusalem, do not weep for me. Weep for yourselves and for your children.* (*Luke* 23:28)—**Hail Mary...**
5. Two others who were criminals were led along with Him to be crucified. (*Lk.* 23:32)—**Hail Mary...**
6. Upon arriving at a site called Golgotha, (a name which means Skull Place), they gave Him a drink of wine flavored with gall, which He tasted but refused to drink. (*Mt.* 27:33-34)—**Hail Mary...**
7. When they had crucified Him, they divided His clothes among them by casting lots; then they sat down there and kept watch over Him. (*Mt.* 27:35-36)—**Hail Mary...**
8. *Whoever wishes to be my follower must deny his very self.* (*Lk.* 9:23)—**Hail Mary...**
9. *He must take up his cross each day and follow in my steps.* (*Lk.* 9:23)—**Hail Mary...**
10. *Whoever would save his life will lose it, whoever loses his life for my sake, will save it.* (*Lk.* 9:24)—**Hail Mary...**

    Glory be to the Father...
    O My Jesus, forgive us our sins...

5. THE CRUCIFIXION

Jesus died on the cross. With it came our redemption, our salvation. Before His final breath, He gave the world His Mother, and gave her a role in the salvation of all mankind by making us all, her children.

Just as she was there, at the foot of the cross, she asks us to pray at the foot of the cross. Our forgiveness is there. Great graces are there. Love the cross. In this meditation, is our salvation.

Prayer Intention

Let us pray for forgiveness and as Jesus forgave on the cross, let us pray for the grace to forgive others. Let us give all our past pain to Jesus. It is why He is on the cross.

Our Father...

1. Jesus said, *Father, forgive them, they do not know what they are doing.* (*Lk.* 23:34)—**Hail Mary...**
2. One of the criminals said: *Jesus, remember me when You enter upon Your reign.* And Jesus replied, *I assure you; this day you will be with Me in paradise.* (*Lk.* 23:42-43)—**Hail Mary...**
3. Seeing His Mother there with the disciple whom He loved, Jesus said to His Mother, *Woman, there is your son.* (*Jn.* 19:26)—**Hail Mary...**
4. In turn He said to the disciple, *There is your Mother.* From that hour onward, the disciple took her into his care. (*Jn.* 19:27)—**Hail Mary...**
5. Then toward midafternoon, Jesus cried out in a loud tone, *My God, My God, why have You forsaken Me?* (*Mt.* 27:46)—**Hail Mary...**
6. Jesus realizing that everything was now finished, said to fulfill the Scriptures, *I am thirsty.* There was a jar there, full of common wine. They stuck a sponge soaked in this wine on a stick, and raised it to His lips. (*Jn.* 19:28)—**Hail Mary...**
7. When Jesus took the wine, He said, *Now it is finished.* (*Jn.* 19:30)—**Hail Mary...**

8. Jesus uttered a loud cry and said, *Father, into Your hands I commend My spirit.* After He said this, He expired. (*Lk.* 23:46)—**Hail Mary...**
9. Darkness came over the whole land until midafternoon with an eclipse of the sun. The curtain in the sanctuary was torn in two. (*Lk.* 23:44-45)—**Hail Mary...**
10. They took Jesus' body, and in accordance with Jewish burial custom, bound it up in wrappings of cloth with perfumed oils. (*Jn.* 19:40)—**Hail Mary...**

Glory be to the Father...
O My Jesus, forgive us our sins...

THE CHAPLET OF MERCY

(To be said on regular rosary beads.)

Begin by saying one each:

Our Father...Hail Mary...The Creed...

On the separated beads say:

Eternal Father, I offer You the Body and Blood, Soul and Divinity of Your dearly beloved Son, Our Lord Jesus Christ, in atonement for our sins and those of the whole world.

On the Hail Mary beads say:

For the sake of His sorrowful Passion, have mercy on us and on the whole world.

Repeat the above for every decade of the rosary. In conclusion say:

Holy God, Holy Mighty One, Holy Immortal One, have mercy on us and on the whole world. (3 times.)

(With Ecclesiastical Permission)

A PRAYER FOR DIVINE MERCY

O Great Merciful God, Infinite Goodness, today all mankind calls out from the abyss of its misery to Your mercy—to Your compassion, O God; and it is with its mighty voice of misery that it cries out. Gracious God, do not reject the prayer of this earth's exiles! O Lord, Goodness beyond our understanding, Who are acquainted with our misery through and through, and know that by our own power we cannot ascend to You, we implore You, anticipate us with Your grace and keep on increasing Your mercy in us, that we may faithfully do Your holy will all through our life and at death's hour. Let the omnipotence of Your mercy shield us from the darts of our salvation's enemies, that we may with confidence, as Your children, await Your final coming—that day known to You alone. And we expect to obtain everything promised us by Jesus, in spite of all our wretchedness, for Jesus is our Hope. Through His merciful Heart, as through an open gate, we pass through to heaven.

(From the Diary of the Servant of God, by Sr. Faustina)
Imprimatur: J. F. Maguire, Bishop of Springfield, MA. Nov. 13, 1979.

LITANY OF THE MOST SACRED HEART OF JESUS

Lord, have mercy on us.
Christ, have mercy on us.
Lord, have mercy on us. Christ hear us.
Christ, graciously hear us.
God the Father of Heaven,
Have mercy on us.
God the Son, Redeemer of the world,
Have mercy on us.
God the Holy Spirit,
Have mercy on us.
Holy Trinity, One God,
Have mercy on us.

Heart of Jesus, Son of the Eternal Father,
(Have mercy on us.)
Heart of Jesus, formed by the Holy Spirit in the womb of the Virgin Mother,
(Have mercy on us.)
Heart of Jesus, substantially united to the Word of God, *(etc.)*
Heart of Jesus, of infinite majesty,
Heart of Jesus, holy Temple of God,
Heart of Jesus, Tabernacle of the Most High,
Heart of Jesus, House of God and Gate of Heaven,
Heart of Jesus, burning Furnace of charity,
Heart of Jesus, Vessel of justice and love,
Heart of Jesus, full of goodness and love,
Heart of Jesus, Abyss of all virtues,
Heart of Jesus, most worthy of all praise,
Heart of Jesus, King and center of all hearts,
Heart of Jesus, in Whom are all the treasures of wisdom and knowledge,
Heart of Jesus, in Whom dwelleth all the fullness of the divinity,

Heart of Jesus, in Whom the Father was well pleased,
Heart of Jesus, of Whose fullness we have all received,
Heart of Jesus, desire of the everlasting hills,
Heart of Jesus, patient and abounding in mercy,
Heart of Jesus, rich unto all who call upon Thee,
Heart of Jesus, Fountain of life and holiness,
Heart of Jesus, Propitiation for our sins,
Heart of Jesus, filled with reproaches,
Heart of Jesus, bruised for our offenses,
Heart of Jesus, obedient unto death,
Heart of Jesus, pierced with a lance,
Heart of Jesus, Source of all consolation,
Heart of Jesus, our Life and Resurrection,
Heart of Jesus, our Peace and Reconciliation,
Heart of Jesus, Victim for our sins,
Heart of Jesus, Salvation of those who hope in Thee,
Heart of Jesus, Hope of those who die in Thee,
Heart of Jesus, Delight of all the saints,

Lamb of God, Who takest away the sins of the world,
Spare us, O Lord.
Lamb of God, Who takest away the sins of the world,
Graciously hear us, O Lord.
Lamb of God, Who takest away the sins of the world,
Have mercy on us.

V. Jesus meek and humble of heart,
R. *Make our hearts like unto Thine.*

Let us pray

Almighty and eternal God, consider the Heart of Your well-beloved Son and the praises and satisfaction He offers You in the name of sinners. Appeased by worthy homage, pardon those who implore Your mercy, in the name of the same Jesus Christ Your Son, Who lives and reigns with You, world without end. Amen.

PART IV

PREPARED FORMAT FOR A SECOND HOUR OF ADORATION

1. THE GLORIOUS MYSTERIES	(15 to 20 min.)
2. PRAYER OR MEDITATION	(10 to 15 min.)
3. CHAPLET OF DIVINE MERCY	(10 min.)
4. OTHER READINGS OR MEDITATION OR LITANY OF THE BLESSED VIRGIN MARY	(10 min.)
5. PRAYERS AND MEDITATION	(10 min.)

VARIOUS MEDITATIONS AVAILABLE IN THIS BOOK:
Part I, page 3.

VARIOUS PRAYERS AVAILABLE IN THIS BOOK:
Part II, page 43.

THE GLORIOUS MYSTERIES

1. THE RESURRECTION

Jesus rose from the dead. With it He conquered death, defeated Satan, sin, and the world, and gave new life to mankind. The joy of the risen Christ is greater than pain. The hope that comes from His resurrection is the victory over our own fear of dying.

Prayer Intention

Let us pray in thanksgiving and in praise, giving glory to the risen Lord. Let us offer to the Triumphant Prince of Peace, all those in despair, those who have lost hope, lost faith; that in the Resurrection of Jesus will be their own future. He is The Way and The Truth and The Life.

Our Father...

1. After the sabbath, as the first day of the week was dawning, Mary Magdalene came with the other Mary to inspect the tomb. (*Mt.* 28:1)—**Hail Mary...**
2. The angel came to the stone, rolled it back and sat on it. (*Mt.* 28:2)—**Hail Mary...**
3. Then the angel spoke, addressing the women: *Do not be frightened. I know you are looking for Jesus the crucified, but He is not here. He has been raised, exactly as He promised.* (*Mt.* 28:5-6)—**Hail Mary...**
4. *He has been raised from the dead and now goes ahead of you to Galilee.* (*Mt.* 28:7)—**Hail Mary...**
5. On the evening of the first day of the week, even though the disciples had locked the doors of the place where they were....Jesus came and stood before

them. *Peace be with you.* He said. (*Jn.* 20:19)—**Hail Mary...**

6. In their panic and fright they thought they were seeing a ghost. (*Lk.* 24:37)—**Hail Mary...**

7. He said to them, *Why are you disturbed? Look at My hands and My feet; it is really I.* (*Lk.* 24:38-39)—**Hail Mary...**

8. At the sight of the Lord, the disciples rejoiced. (*Jn.* 20:20)—**Hail Mary...**

9. *Peace be with you.* Jesus said again. *As the Father has sent Me, so I send you.* (*Jn.* 20:21)—**Hail Mary...**

10. *I am the resurrection and the life; whoever believes in Me, though he should die, will come to life.* (*Jn.* 11:25-26)—**Hail Mary...**

Glory be to the Father...
O My Jesus, forgive us our sins...

2. THE ASCENSION

He goes to prepare a place for us, and has returned to The Father, in heaven. And He has promised: *Where I am, you can be too.* Through His ascension, He has shown us a preview of our life hereafter. The Good Shepherd guides us through the valley of darkness.

Prayer Intention

Let us pray for direction; direction in our lives and for all those who have lost the way; that they may turn back to God. Let us pray that we might give direction to the children in the world, that Jesus may become their first priority.

Our Father...

1. Jesus led His disciples out near Bethany, and with

hands upraised, blessed them. (*Lk.* 24:50)—**Hail Mary...**

2. Jesus addressed them in these words: *Full authority has been given to Me both in heaven and on earth.* (*Mt.* 28:18)—**Hail Mary...**
3. *Go therefore, and make disciples of all the nations. Baptize them in the name of the Father, and of the Son, and of the Holy Spirit.* (*Mt.* 28:19)—**Hail Mary...**
4. *And know that I am with you always, until the end of the world.* (*Mt.* 28:20)—**Hail Mary...**
5. *The man who believes in the good news and accepts baptism will be saved; the man who refuses to believe in it will be condemned...* (*Mk.* 16:16)—**Hail Mary...**
6. As Jesus blessed them, He left them and was taken up to heaven. (*Lk.* 24:51)—**Hail Mary...**
7. He was lifted up before their eyes in a cloud which took Him from their sight. (*Acts.* 1:9)—**Hail Mary...**
8. This Jesus Who has been taken from you will return, just as you saw Him go up into the heavens. (*Acts.* 1:11)—**Hail Mary...**
9. They fell down to do Him reverence, then returned to Jerusalem filled with joy. (*Lk.* 24:52)—**Hail Mary...**
10. Jesus took His seat at God's right hand. (*Mk.* 16:19)—**Hail Mary...**
    Glory be to the Father...
    O My Jesus, forgive us our sins...

3. THE DESCENT OF THE HOLY SPIRIT

Before His Ascension, Jesus had said, *Because I go, the Paraclete will come.* The Spirit of God descended upon the apostles. They were empowered with the special gifts of God, to carry on the Lord's work of redemption. With them, was Mary, and the other women, praying with the infant Church. She has never ceased to pray for us and the Church.

Prayer Intention

Let us offer these prayers for our own penticost. For an increase in the Holy Spirit's gifts to us. We pray for a deeper faith, and trust in God; for a complete submission to the will of God. Let us pray especially for gifts to the young, that they may be able to stand up to the deception Satan brings to their daily activities.

Our Father...

1. Jesus said, *I will ask the Father and He will give you another Paraclete, to be with you always.* (*Jn.* 14:16)—**Hail Mary...**
2. *The Paraclete, the Holy Spirit, whom the Father will send in My name, will instruct you in everything, and remind you of all that I told you.* (*Jn.* 14:26)—**Hail Mary...**
3. *Within a few days you will be baptized with the Holy Spirit.* (*Acts.* 1:5)—**Hail Mary...**
4. *You will receive power when the Holy Spirit comes down on you; then you are to be My witnesses in Jerusalem, throughout Judea....and even to the ends of the earth.* (*Acts.* 1:8)—**Hail Mary...**
5. When the day of Pentecost came it found them gathered in one place. Suddenly from up in the sky there came a noise like a strong driving wind, which was heard all through the house. (*Acts.* 2:1-2)—**Hail Mary...**
6. Tongues as of fire appeared, which parted and came to rest on each of them. All were filled with the Holy Spirit. (*Acts.* 2:3)—**Hail Mary...**

7. They began to express themselves in foreign tongues and make bold proclamation as the Spirit prompted them. (*Acts.* 2:4)—**Hail Mary...**
8. Staying in Jerusalem at the time were devout men of every nation. These heard the sound, and assembled in a large crowd. They were confused because each heard the disciples speaking his own language. (*Acts.* 2:5-6)—**Hail Mary...**
9. Peter stood up with the Eleven and addressed them, *You must reform and be baptized, each one of you, in the name of Jesus Christ, that your sins may be forgiven; then you will receive the gift of the Holy Spirit.* (*Acts.* 2:38)—**Hail Mary...**
10. Those who accepted His message were baptized; some three thousand were added that day. (*Acts.* 2:41)—**Hail Mary...**

Glory be to the Father...
O My Jesus, forgive us our sins...

4. THE ASSUMPTION

Mary is assumed body and soul into heaven. Reunited with her Son, Jesus. Through her assumption, Mary became the reflection of her risen Son. She is also the model of the perfection to which we are called.

Prayer Intention

Here let us ask Mary to especially pray with us for the souls in purgatory; that she might join with us in intercession for those who can no longer help themselves. Let us pray especially for the souls forgotten, who have no one to remember them.

Our Father...

1. The Lord God said to the serpent: *I will put enmity between you and the woman and between your off-*

spring and hers. (*Gn.* 3:15)—**Hail Mary...**

2. *He will strike at your head, while you strike at His heel.* (*Gn.* 3:15)—**Hail Mary...**

3. A great sign appeared in the sky, a woman clothed with the sun, with the moon under her feet, and on her head a crown of twelve stars. (*Rv.* 12:1)—**Hail Mary...**

4. *Father, all those you gave me I would have in my company where I am.* (*Jn.* 17:24)—**Hail Mary...**

5. Wherefore she is our Mother in the order of grace. (*Vat. II, Constit.* on Ch. 61)—**Hail Mary...**

6. Taken up to heaven, she did not lay aside this salvific duty, but by her intercession continues to bring us the gifts of eternal salvation. (*Vat. II, Constit.* of Ch. 62)—**Hail Mary...**

7. *For He has looked upon His servant in her lowliness.* (*Lk.* 1:48)—**Hail Mary...**

8. *All ages to come shall call me blessed.* (*Lk.* 1:48)—**Hail Mary...**

9. Those who love me I also love, and those who seek me find me. . .He who finds me finds life, and wins favor from the Lord. (*Prov.* 8:17-35)—**Hail Mary...**

10. Come then my love. My lovely one come. (*Song* 2:10)—**Hail Mary...**

Glory be to the Father...
O My Jesus, forgive us our sins...

5. THE CORONATION OF MARY

Mary is crowned Queen of the angels and saints in heaven. Queen of the Holy Rosary, Queen of Peace, Queen of Apostles, Queen of Prophets. How many titles have been given to the Mother of the Incarnation of the Word! Her soul magnifies the Lord, all nations shall call her blessed. Her glorious coronation in heaven, is our hope.

Prayer Intention

Let us offer this mystery then for Mary's intentions. Her intercession, her constant appearances, her role as Mediatrix of graces. Let us pray that her efforts in our behalf, her efforts to lead all her children back to her Son, will not be impeded.

Our Father...

1. *God who is mighty, has done great things for me.* (*Lk.* 1:49)—**Hail Mary...**
2. My heart overflows with a goodly theme; as I sing my ode to the king. (*Ps.* 45:2)—**Hail Mary...**
3. Fairer in beauty are you than the sons of men; grace is poured out upon your lips; thus God has blessed you forever. (*Ps.* 45:3)—**Hail Mary...**
4. Because of this gift of sublime grace, she far surpasses all creatures, both in heaven and on earth. (*Vat. II, Constit.* of Ch. 53)—**Hail Mary...**
5. I am the rose of Sharon, I am the lily of the valleys. (*Song* 2:1)—**Hail Mary...**
6. So now, O children, listen to me; instruction and wisdom do not reject. (*Prov.* 8:32-33)—**Hail Mary...**
7. The Lord chose her. He chose her before she was born. (*Div. off.*)—**Hail Mary...**
8. Entirely holy, and free from all stain of sin. (*Constit.* of Ch. 56)—**Hail Mary...**

9. Freely cooperating in the work of human salvation through faith and obedience. (*Constit.* of Ch. 56)—**Hail Mary...**

10. Blessed are you, daughter, by the Most High God, above all the women on earth. (*Judith* 13:18)—**Hail Mary...**

Glory be to the Father...
O My Jesus, forgive us our sins...

Prayer After the Rosary

O, God, whose only-begotten Son, by His life, death and resurrection, has purchased for us the rewards of eternal life; grant, we beseech Thee, that, meditating upon these mysteries of the Most Holy Rosary of the Blessed Virgin Mary, we may imitate what they contain and obtain what they promise, through the same Christ Our Lord. Amen.

May the Divine Assistance remain always with us. And may the souls of the faithful departed, through the mercy of God, rest in peace. Amen.

THE LITANY OF THE BLESSED VIRGIN MARY

Lord have mercy on us.
Christ, have mercy on us.
Lord, have mercy on us. Christ, hear us.
Christ, graciously hear us.
God the Father of Heaven,
Have mercy on us.
God the Son, Redeemer of the world,
Have mercy on us.
God the Holy Spirit,
Have mercy on us.
Holy Trinity, One God,
Have mercy on us.

Holy Mary, *(pray for us).*
Holy Mother of God, *(pray for us).*
Holy Virgin of virgins, *(etc.).*
Mother of Christ,
Mother of divine grace,
Mother most pure,
Mother most chaste,
Mother inviolate,
Mother undefiled,
Mother most amiable,
Mother most admirable,
Mother of good counsel,
Mother of our Creator,
Mother of our Saviour,
Mother of the Church,
Virgin most prudent,
Virgin most venerable,
Virgin most renowned,
Virgin most powerful,
Virgin most merciful,
Virgin most faithful,
Mirror of justice,

Seat of wisdom,
Cause of our joy,
Spiritual vessel,
Vessel of honor,
Singular vessel of devotion,
Mystical rose,
Tower of David,
Tower of ivory,
House of gold,
Ark of the covenant,
Gate of Heaven,
Morning star,
Health of the sick,
Refuge of sinners,
Comforter of the afflicted,
Help of Christians,
Queen of angels,
Queen of patriarchs,
Queen of prophets,
Queen of apostles,
Queen of martyrs,
Queen of confessors,
Queen of virgins,
Queen of all saints,
Queen conceived without Original Sin,
Queen assumed into Heaven,
Queen of the most holy Rosary,
Queen of peace,

Lamb of God, Who takest away the sins of the world,
Spare us, O Lord.
Lamb of God, Who takest away the sins of the world,
Graciously hear us, O Lord.
Lamb of God, Who takest away the sins of the world,
Have mercy on us.

V. Pray for us, O Holy Mother of God,
R. *That we may be made worthy of the promises of Christ.*

THE JOYFUL MYSTERIES

1. THE ANNUNCIATION

The Annunciation is a symbol of humility, of submission to the will of God. Here, Mary receives the message from the angel that she will bear the Redeemer of the world. Mary's faith, her submission becomes our model. She asks for our submission to God as well.

Prayer Intention

Our Lady would want us to pray for humility, for submission to God's will. Let us offer this first decade of the rosary, in reparation; in reparation for all who revolt against God's will, against the call of their own conscience. Let us pray especially for the Church, for all bishops, priests and all those in religious life, that they might serve God with humility and imitate Mary, the "Model of the Church, the Mother of the Church."

Our Father...

1. The Angel Gabriel was sent from God. . . . to a virgin betrothed to a man, named Joseph, of the House of David. The virgin's name was Mary. (*Lk.* 1:26)— **Hail Mary...**
2. The angel said to her: *Rejoice O highly favored daughter! The Lord is with you. Blessed are you among women.* (*Lk.*1:28)—**Hail Mary...**
3. She was deeply troubled by his words, and wondered what his greeting meant. (*Lk.* 1:29)—**Hail Mary...**
4. The angel said to her: *Do not fear, Mary. You have found favor with God.* (*Lk.* 1:30)—**Hail Mary...**

5. *You shall conceive and bear a Son and give Him the name of Jesus.* (*Lk.* 1:31)—**Hail Mary...**
6. *Great will be His dignity and He will be called Son of the Most High. And His reign will be without end.* (*Lk.* 1:32-33)—**Hail Mary...**
7. Mary said to the angel, *How can this be since I do not know man?* (*Lk.* 1:34)—**Hail Mary...**
8. The angel answered her: *The Holy Spirit will come upon you and the power of the Most High will overshadow you.* (*Lk.* 1:35)—**Hail Mary...**
9. *The holy offspring to be born will be called Son of God.* (*Lk.* 1:35)—**Hail Mary...**
10. Mary said: *I am the servant of the Lord. Let it be done to me as you say.* With that the angel left her. (*Lk.* 1:38)—**Hail Mary...**

Glory be to the Father...
Oh My Jesus, forgive us our sins...

2. THE VISITATION

Mary came to Elizabeth, to visit with her relative. She came with a stirring message concerning the nearness of Our Saviour. The Incarnation of the Word was upon us. Listen to Mary's prayer of praise to God, "The Magnificat."

Prayer Intention

Let us pray this decade in thanksgiving; in thanks to God for coming to us through Mary—for greater recognition of her role, her acceptance of God's will.

Our Father...

1. Mary set out, proceeding in haste into the hill country to a town of Judah, where she entered Zechariah's house and greeted Elizabeth. (*Lk.* 1:39-40)—**Hail Mary...**

2. When Elizabeth heard Mary's greeting, the baby leapt in her womb. (*Lk.* 1:41)—**Hail Mary...**

3. Elizabeth was filled with the Holy Spirit. (*Lk.* 1:41)—**Hail Mary...**

4. She cried out in a loud voice: *Blessed are you among women and blest is the fruit of your womb.* (*Lk.* 1:42)—**Hail Mary...**

5. *Blest is she who trusted that the Lord's words to her would be fulfilled.* (*Lk.* 1:45)—**Hail Mary...**

6. Then Mary said: *My being proclaims the greatness of the Lord, my spirit finds joy in God my Saviour.* (*Lk.* 1:46-47)—**Hail Mary...**

7. *For He has looked upon His servant in her lowliness; all ages to come shall call me blessed.* (*Lk.* 1:48)—**Hail Mary...**

8. *God who is mighty has done great things for me, holy is His name.* (*Lk.* 1:49)—**Hail Mary...**

9. *His mercy is from age to age on those who fear Him.* (*Lk.* 1:50)—**Hail Mary...**

10. Mary remained with Elizabeth about three months and then returned home. (*Lk.* 1:56)—**Hail Mary...**

Glory be to the Father...
Oh My Jesus, forgive us our sins...

3. THE NATIVITY

He is with us. The word was made flesh and now Jesus Christ is with us. What impact does that have on us today? He came not as a King, or a ruler, but as a poor infant, born in a manger, accompanied by shepherds. And to such humble beginnings, every knee must bend. What gifts do we bring? Bring joy, bring love and praise. Give your heart. Give your trust as Joseph did.

Prayer Intention

Let us pray for families, for guidance and grace to imitate the Holy Family. Let us pray for all parents and all those who care for the young. Let us pray especially for the gift of life, and all those who cherish it; for parents that they will lead their children closer to God. Let us pray for the unborn and in reparation for those who rob the unborn of the gift of life.

Our Father...

1. Suddenly the angel of the Lord appeared in a dream, and said to him: *Joseph, son of David, have no fear....It is by the Holy Spirit that she has conceived this child.* (*Mt.* 1:20)—**Hail Mary...**

2. *She is to have a son and you are to name Him Jesus, because He will save His people from their sins.* (*Mt.* 1:21)—**Hail Mary...**

3. All this happened to fulfill what the Lord has said through the prophet: *The virgin shall be with Child and give birth to a Son, and they shall call Him Emmanuel, a name which means 'God is with us.'* (*Mt.* 1:22-24)—**Hail Mary...**

4. In those days Caesar Augustus published a decree ordering a census of the whole world. And so Joseph went to Judea, to David's town of Bethlehem—because he was of the house and lineage of David—to register with Mary, his espoused wife, who was with Child. (*Lk.* 2:1), (*Lk.* 2:4-5)—**Hail Mary...**
5. While they were there the days of her confinement were completed. She gave birth to her first-born Son and wrapped Him in swaddling clothes and laid Him in a manger. (*Lk.* 2:6-7)—**Hail Mary...**
6. There were shepherds in that region, living in the fields and keeping night watch. . . . over their flocks. (*Lk.* 2:8)—**Hail Mary...**
7. The angel of the Lord appeared to them and they were very much afraid. The angel said to them: *You have nothing to fear.* (*Lk.* 2:9-10)—**Hail Mary...**
8. *I come to proclaim good news to you—tidings of great joy. This day in David's city a Saviour has been born to you, The Messiah and Lord.* (*Lk.* 2:10-11)—**Hail Mary...**
9. Suddenly there was with the angel a multitude of the heavenly host, praising God and saying: *Glory to God in high heaven, peace on earth to those on whom His favor rests.* (*Lk.* 2:13-14)—**Hail Mary...**
10. They went in haste and found Mary and Joseph, and the Baby lying in the manger; once they saw, they understood what had been told them concerning this Child. (*Lk.* 2:16-17)—**Hail Mary...**

Glory be to the Father...
Oh My Jesus, forgive us our sins...

4. THE PRESENTATION

Mary and Joseph, in compliance with the laws of their land, brought the infant Jesus to the temple for consecration to God the Father. She is still presenting Him to us, everyday. Offering her Son everyday to us, through the Mass, through His graces, His blessings. She also attempts to present us to God everyday; to dress us in holiness, goodness, obedience and humility for presentation to her Son.

Prayer Intention

Let us pray this decade for Mary's intentions. That all of her children may accept her role as intercessor in preparing us to be worthy of presentation to her Son, Our Saviour.

Our Father...

1. When the day came to purify them according to the law of Moses, the couple brought Him up to Jerusalem so that He could be presented to the Lord. (*Lk.* 2:22)—**Hail Mary...**

2. There lived in Jerusalem at the time a certain man named Simeon. He was just and pious. . . .and the Holy Spirit was upon him. (*Lk.* 2:25)—**Hail Mary...**

3. It was revealed to him by the Holy Spirit that he would not experience death until he had seen the Anointed of the Lord. (*Lk.* 2:26)—**Hail Mary...**

4. He came to the temple now, inspired by the Spirit, and when the parents brought in the Child Jesus, he took Him in his arms and blessed God. (*Lk.* 2:27-28)—**Hail Mary...**

5. *Now Master, You can dismiss Your servant in peace; You have fulfilled Your word.* (*Lk.* 2:29)—**Hail Mary...**

6. *For my eyes have witnessed your saving deed, displayed for all the peoples to see.* (*Lk.* 2:30-31)—**Hail Mary...**

7. Simeon blessed them and said to Mary His Mother; *This Child is destined to be the downfall and the rise of many in Israel, a sign that will be opposed.* (*Lk.* 2:34)—**Hail Mary...**

8. *And you yourself shall be pierced with a sword—so that the thoughts of many hearts may be laid bare.* (*Lk.* 2:35)—**Hail Mary...**

9. When the pair had fulfilled all the prescriptions of the law of the Lord, they returned to Galilee and their own town of Nazareth. (*Lk.* 2:39)—**Hail Mary...**

10. The Child grew in size and strength, filled with wisdom, and the grace of God was upon Him. (*Lk.* 2:40)—**Hail Mary...**

Glory be to the Father...
O My Jesus, forgive us our sins...

5. THE FINDING OF JESUS IN THE TEMPLE

Mary and Joseph searched in sorrow for three days before they experienced the joy of finding Jesus. She is still searching today for all of her lost children. Do we see in this event, an example of the constant need to search for the lost?

Prayer Intention

Let us offer this decade for conversion. For all those who have wandered away from God; for those who have lost their faith; for those who give their life to the false gods of the world, money, materialism, and pleasure.

Our Father. . .

1. And when He was twelve they went up for the celebration as was their custom. (*Lk.* 2:42)—**Hail Mary. . .**
2. As they were returning at the end of the feast, the Child Jesus remained behind unknown to His parents. (*Lk.* 2:43)—**Hail Mary. . .**
3. Thinking He was in the party, they continued their journey for a day, looking for Him among their relatives and acquaintances. (*Lk.* 2:44)—**Hail Mary. . .**
4. Not finding Him, they returned to Jerusalem in search of Him. (*Lk.* 2:45)—**Hail Mary. . .**
5. On the third day they came upon Him in the temple sitting in the midst of the teachers. . . . All who heard Him were amazed at His intelligence and His answers. (*Lk.* 2:46-47)—**Hail Mary. . .**
6. And His Mother said to Him: *Son, why have You done this to us? You see that Your father and I have been searching for You in sorrow.* (*Lk.* 2:48)—**Hail Mary. . .**
7. He said to them; *"Why did you search for me? Did you not know I had to be in My Father's house?*

(*Lk.* 2:49)—**Hail Mary...**

8. But they did not grasp what He said to them. (*Lk.* 2:50)—**Hail Mary...**
9. He went down with them then, and came to Nazareth, and was obedient to them. (*Lk.* 2:51)—**Hail Mary...**
10. His Mother meanwhile, kept all these things in memory. Jesus, for His part, progressed steadily in wisdom and age and grace before God and men. (*Lk.* 2:52)—**Hail Mary...**

    Glory be to the Father...
    Oh My Jesus, forgive us our sins...

ADDITIONAL TITLES AVAILABLE ON PRAYER

Contact The Riehle Foundation

WHY PRAYER? AND HOW TO PRAY

by Fr. René Laurentin

A brilliant yet simple look at prayer. Fr. Laurentin reminds us of the often forgotten truth: "God is the Creator; we are the created," the only existence which gives meaning to everything else.

104 pages **$4.00**

THE POWER OF THE ROSARY

by Fr. Albert J. Shamon

Historical instances of how praying the rosary has been a powerful weapon for peace. Suggestions on how to meditate, and many reasons why the Rosary prayer is so powerful.

48 pages **$2.00**

(Also available in Spanish)
El Poder Del Rosario

PRIMER OF PRAYER

by Fr. Bartholomew J. O'Brien

Provides the basics on prayer and progresses to address the different types of prayer: vocal, spontaneous, meditative and contemplative.

124 pages **$3.00**

THE HAIL MARY
ITS MEANING AND ITS ORIGIN
by Fr. René Laurentin

The rich tradition of this beautiful prayer explained in-depth, its origin and development. The basis for the meditation it can inspire; the explanation why the Blessed Virgin Mary merits our most special attention.

96 pages **$4.00**

A WOMAN OF MANY TITLES
by Fr. Charles Mangan

An outline, synopsis, meditation and concluding prayer for many of the titles given to Mary. A beautiful and prayer-filled book. Contains 14 color pictures of Icons and famous works of art depicting Mary under her various titles.

64 pages **$4.00**

OUR LADY TEACHES ABOUT PRAYER AT MEDJUGORJE
by Fr. Albert J. Shamon

This beautiful booklet outlines Our Lady's teachings about prayer and the need for prayer in our everyday living. Over 160,000 copies distributed.

64 pages **$1.00**

(Also available in Spanish)

La Virgin Nos Ensena A Orar

THE RIEHLE FOUNDATION...

The Riehle Foundation is a non-profit, tax-exempt, charitable organization that exists to produce and/or distribute Catholic material to anyone, anywhere.

The Foundation is dedicated to the Mother of God and her role in the salvation of mankind. We believe that this role has not diminished in our time, but, on the contrary has become all the more apparent in this the era of Mary as recognized by Pope John Paul II, whom we strongly support.

During the past five years the foundation has distributed over four million books, films, rosaries, bibles, etc. to individuals, parishes, and organizations all over the world. Additionally, the foundation sends materials to missions and parishes in a dozen foreign countries.

Donations forwarded to The Riehle Foundation for the materials distributed provide our sole support. We appreciate your assistance, and request your prayers.

For copies of the books listed here, or for a catalog, contact:

The Riehle Foundation
P.O. Box 7
Milford, OH 45150
513-576-0032